What teen girls have to say about *The Inside Story*

This is such an amazing book. A lot of the questions are ones I would have asked myself. I definitely showed it to my mom, too. It has improved our relationship a ton! It's a great book.

—*Erin, age 15*

My mom and I both read this book, and we loved it! Our mother–daughter relationship has had its ups and downs, but this book is an excellent resource for opening up conversations and understanding the stresses both of us face.

—*Emily, age 16*

This is a perfect book for adolescent girls. It builds self-confidence and helps girls realize that they are not the only ones who are confused about themselves. Girls will see that many other teens have the same problems and questions as they do, and this book can help answer them.

—*Toby, age 17, featured in the film 5 Girls televised on PBS*

The Inside Story on Teen Girls

The Inside Story on Teen Girls

Story
on
Teen Girls

Experts Answer **Teens'** Questions

**Karen Zager, PhD, and
Alice Rubenstein, EdD**

**APA
LifeTools**

American Psychological Association • Washington, DC

Published by
American Psychological Association
750 First Street, NE
Washington, DC 20002
www.apa.org

To order	Tel: (800) 374-2721, Direct: (202) 336-5510
APA Order Department	Fax: (202) 336-5502, TDD/TTY: (202) 336-6123
P.O. Box 92984	On-line: www.apa.org/books/
Washington, DC 20090-2984	E-mail: order@apa.org

In the U.K., Europe, Africa, and the Middle East, copies may be ordered from
American Psychological Association
3 Henrietta Street
Covent Garden, London
WC2E 8LU England

Typeset in Minion by EPS Group Inc., Easton, MD

Printer: Phoenix Color Corporation, Hagerstown, MD
Cover Designer: Naylor Design, Washington, DC
Technical/Production Editor: Jennifer L. Macomber

The opinions and statements published are the responsibility of the authors, and such opinions and statements do not necessarily represent the policies of the American Psychological Association.

Library of Congress Cataloging-in-Publication Data
Zager, Karen (Karen M.)
    The inside story on teen girls / by Karen Zager and Alice Rubenstein.— 1st ed.
        p. cm.
    ISBN 1-55798-892-7 (alk. paper)
    1. Teenage girls.   2. Adolescence.   3. Parent and teenager.
I. Rubenstein, Alice K.   II. Title.

HQ798 .Z34 2002
305.235—dc21

                                                                    2002020532

British Library Cataloguing-in-Publication Data
A CIP record is available from the British Library.

Printed in the United States of America
First Edition

To our significant others, Howard and Andy, for supporting us, loving us, and putting up with us during years of research and writing.

To our children, Erik, Russell, Heather, and Jennifer, for challenging us and keeping us truthful, honest, and humble.

To our mothers, Eleanor and Gertrude, who nurtured us through our own adolescence and who continue to love and guide us.

And to our fathers, Harold and Paul, who celebrated us as daughters and women and who remained young at heart throughout their lives.

We are so grateful to you all.—*Karen and Alice*

Your new life is, and has begun—
Live it to the fullest,
You have earned it,
And deserve that and more.

Herbert J. Freudenberger, 1982

Contents

Acknowledgments

This book was a labor of love and would not have been "born" without the assistance and support of many friends and colleagues:

- Julia Frank-McNeil, our editor and Director of APA Books, who steadfastly believed in the project and provided unending help and encouragement throughout.
- Gary R. VandenBos, PhD, APA Publisher, who made the idea of this book a possibility and who stood by us every step of the way.
- Dr. Dorothy Cantor, APA Past President, for having the wisdom and foresight to convene a Task Force on Adolescent Girls and provide us with the forum from which this project emerged.
- Dr. Norine Johnson, Co-chair of the Task Force on Adolescent Girls and APA Past President, for her

friendship, insight, and commitment to recognizing and supporting the strengths and resiliency of adolescent girls.

- Dara Querimit, our graduate research assistant, who volunteered so generously of her time, energy, and ideas.
- Mary Campbell, APA Children, Youth, and Families Officer, who was a calming and reassuring anchor, as well as an invaluable source of information and coordination during the research phase of the project.
- Gabriele S. Clune, Manager of the Task Force on Adolescent Girls, who also provided staff support.
- Jessica Kohout, PhD, Director of the APA Research Office, who provided the research expertise for the data analysis.
- TOPSS (Teachers of Psychology in the Secondary Schools), who distributed the survey questions to adolescents and parents across the country and without whose help and support this book could never have been written.
- The hundreds of teens and parents who responded to our survey and asked us the questions that form the core of this book.
- The adolescents and their parents who have sought out our professional help, trusted us with their innermost thoughts and feelings, and from whom we have learned so very much. You have truly been our best teachers.
- And, of course, our deepest gratitude goes to our

panel of experts, who gave so generously of their time and contributed their psychological knowledge, perspective, and expertise. By providing us with their unique perspectives to the questions raised by hundreds of teens and their parents, they have ensured that this book reflects a diversity of experience and background and a breadth of psychological knowledge that can come only from having so many "coauthors." Our panel included

Carolyn Anderson, PhD, Rochester, NY
Andrea Bastiani Archibald, PhD, New York, NY
Terri A. Betts, PsyD, Boston, MA
Bonnie L. Blankmeyer, PhD, San Antonio, TX
Dorella L. Bond, PhD, Glastonbury, CT
Jeanne Brooks-Gunn, PhD, New York, NY
Cheryl R. Buechner, PhD, Cumberland, WI
Ann F. Caron, EdD, Greenwich, CT
Nancyann N. Cervantes, PhD, JD, Marietta, OH
Catherine S. Chilman, PhD, Mitchellville, MD
W. James Cosse, PhD, Hartsdale, NY
Lisa K. Desai, PsyD, Brookline, MA
Kunya Des Jardins, PhD, Brighton, MA
Baruch Fischhoff, PhD, Pittsburgh, PA
Bruce M. Gilberg, PhD, Rochester, NY
Julia A. Graber, PhD, New York, NY
Kate F. Hays, PhD, Toronto, Ontario, Canada
Kristen Vaughan Huntley, PhD, River Vale, NJ
Yo Jackson, PhD, Lawrence, KS
Norine G. Johnson, PhD, Boston, MA
Judith V. Jordan, PhD, Lexington, MA
Laura Kastner, PhD, Seattle, WA

Howard A. Liddle, EdD, Miami, FL
Jackson Rainer, PhD, Boiling Springs, NC
Susan K. Riesch, DNSc, Madison, WI
Sharon Scales Rostosky, PhD, Lexington, KY
Dee L. Shepherd-Look, PhD, Northridge, CA
Peter L. Sheras, PhD, Charlottesville, VA
Sandra Sims-Patterson, PhD, Atlanta, GA
Dominicus W. So, PhD, Washington, DC
Sheilla St-Fleurose, PsyD, Roslindale, MA
Deborah L. Tolman, EdD, Wellesley, MA
Richard B. Weinberg, PhD, Tampa, FL
Deborah Welsh, PhD, Knoxville, TN

About the Authors

Karen Zager, PhD, is a psychologist in private practice in New York, specializing in adolescence, parenting, and relationship issues. She was featured in the MTV *Warning Signs* anti-violence video and consulted on the PBS documentary film *5 Girls*. She has been interviewed for dozens of magazines and newspapers, including *USA Today*, *The Washington Post*, *The Wall Street Journal*, *Ladies Home Journal*, *Parent Magazine*, *Cosmo Girl*, *Time*, and *Mademoiselle*, and is a regular contributor to *YM Magazine*. She has frequently been interviewed on TV (*Good Morning America*, CBS Eyewitness News, Fox 5 News, *The O'Reilly Report*, *The Donohue Show*, and *Sally Jesse Raphael*), as well as on the radio and Web sites to discuss topics of adolescence and parenting. She was the recipient of the American Psychological Association (APA) Presidential Citation for contributions to the field of psychology and the Distinguished Psychologist of the Year Award from Psychologists in Independent Practice of the APA. She served as co-chair of the APA Presidential Task Force on Adolescent Girls and was President of Psychologists in Independent Practice, a Division of the APA. She is also a wife and the proud mother of two teenagers.

Alice Rubenstein, EdD, is a psychologist in private practice in upstate New York and the mother of two terrific girls. She is founder and partner in the Monroe Psychotherapy and Consultation Center, where she provides individual, family, and relationship counseling. For the past 25 years, much of her work has focused on adolescents and parenting, including consultation with schools and community agencies that serve teens and their families. She is a core consultant to the U.S. Department of Health and Human Services Office of Adolescent Health and served as a consultant to the PBS documentary film *5 Girls*. She is frequently interviewed by the radio and print media, including *Newsweek*, *Shape*, *Self*, *Sassy*, and the new Health Scout Web site.

Dr. Rubenstein has served on the American Psychological Association (APA) Presidential Task Force on Adolescents Girls, as well as the Task Force on Women and Depression. As Director of the APA Division of Psychotherapy Brochure Project, she has spearheaded the development of a series of public information brochures that address issues of concern to both parents and professionals who work with teens. These include *Attention Deficit Disorder in Children and Adolescents* and *A Parent's Guide to Psychotherapy with Children and Adolescents*. She was chosen as the Distinguished Speaker by the APA Office of Continuing Education and is the author of numerous articles and book chapters on how to understand, communicate, and work with adolescents. She is the recipient of the Distinguished Psychologist Award from the Division of Psychotherapy of the APA and has served as President of the Division.

Introduction

So What Is "Normal" Anyway?

The truth is, there is no one single or simple answer to the question "What is normal?" What is "normal" for you depends on things like your age, your culture, your family background, your religious beliefs, your peer group, and even your unique talents, interests, and personal values. So, what is normal can really mean a lot of different things. What is typical in one family might be very unusual in another family. For example, your friend might talk easily to her parents about dating and sex, but you might not even be able to mention the word "sex" without your parents freaking out.

As psychologists who love working with teens, we have talked to hundreds of adolescent girls about their worries and concerns, successes and failures, struggles and dreams. The girls we spoke to convinced us that to navigate the sometimes wild river of adolescence, teen girls needed more information and ideas about how to handle the challenges and choices that go along with being a normal teen.

So, we decided to write a book that would directly help teen girls like you and maybe even your parents and teachers. We didn't want to *assume* that we knew what adolescent girls wanted to know, we wanted to ask them directly. And we did just that. We asked teens from all over the United States the following question: "If you had the chance to have a private and confidential conversation with an expert with a great deal of knowledge and understanding about the concerns of adolescent girls today, what would you ask them?"

The teens we surveyed come from almost every racial, ethnic, and religious group in the country. Some of them live in cities, some in the suburbs, and others in small towns or in the countryside. Some of their families are rich, some just average, and others have very little money. As a group, the teens asked us over 6,000 questions. To our surprise, it did not seem to matter very much what their race, ethnic background, or religion was—or even where they lived or how much money their family had. In the end, they had many similar questions. While we would have loved to answer every question, they would simply not all fit into this one book. So, we chose those questions that were asked the most often.

Of all the thousands of questions we were asked, by far the ones that kept popping up the most were questions about what is "normal." A 16-year-old asked, "What is the borderline between normal and abnormal?" A 13-year-old wanted to know, "Do all adolescent girls my age have the same problems?" And a 15-year-old asked, "What are the most common problems that adolescent girls face?" And so, first we thought it was very important to talk about "normal" as it relates to teen girls. Take a minute and think about what *you* consider to be normal. For example, do you think it's normal to argue with your parents? Is it normal to drink or use drugs? Is it normal to have a steady boyfriend? Is it normal to want to spend lots of time alone in your room?

As we thought about how to answer these and all the other questions, we realized that almost every question could have more than one *answer*. So, we decided to bring together a panel of experts from all over the country, from many different backgrounds and work settings. We asked each of them to give us their ideas about how they would answer the questions. In this way, the answers we have given you include the very best suggestions from almost 50 experts. In this book, you'll find tons of ideas about how to deal with all sorts of problems and concerns.

As you read this book, keep in mind that just as there is no one meaning to the word "normal," there is no one right answer to most of the questions. This is why we have given you several answers to almost every question. You will get the most out of this book if you read all of the answers to a question and take some time to think about your unique background and circumstances to see which answers might be most helpful to you. Remember to be open-minded, and don't be afraid to try something different. You'll find many new ideas and great tips in this book. But, you won't know if something will work for you unless you try it.

Being an adolescent girl today can be very stressful. We think this book will help you a lot. And, don't forget to take a peek at the flip side of this book. Find out what your parents want to know about you and what the experts are telling them.

The Inside Story on Teen Girls

1

Who Am I?
And Why Do I Feel This Way?

I feel so moody and stressed out. I'm so sensitive about everything. Sometimes, I don't even feel like doing stuff that I usually enjoy. Yesterday, I just blew up, and then I felt so lousy about myself. My moods are like a roller coaster, up and down, up and down. Sometimes my family looks at me like I'm crazy. They expect me to be able to handle all the pressures. Guys don't seem to have so many problems. It just isn't fair. I wish I could handle stuff better.— *Yvonne*

Why am I stressed all the time? *Nancy, age 19*

"Stress" is one of the words most frequently used by teens today to describe how hard it is to juggle and balance all the demands on them. When you were a kid, there were, most likely, far fewer demands on you. As you get older, not only do you have many more pressures and responsibilities, but you have many more decisions to make. Teens today are being asked to do so many things—succeed in school, get involved in after-school activities, do volunteer work, hold a part-time job, spend time with friends and family. There are just not enough hours in the day, so you feel "stressed out"! And, as you move toward graduating from high school, there are even tougher issues to deal with, like "What shall I do after high school—go to work or college?" "I want to move out on my own; will I be able to afford it?" "I really love my boyfriend, but I want to have some time to explore myself and the world, and he wants me to stay around for him." With all this stuff to deal with, who wouldn't be stressed?

Now is the time to begin learning how to cope with stress. Here are some things you can try. Physical exercise is a great stress reducer and good for your health. Get some relaxation tapes from your local library, and learn some great relaxation techniques. Yoga or meditation can help, too. Whatever you decide on, do something. Too much stress not only takes the fun out of life but can also have a negative effect on your physical health.

* * *

The answer to why you are stressed is simple: because there probably *is* a lot of stress in your life. There are all the demands of school: papers, projects, homework assignments, and exams. Maybe even

SATs, college applications, or job hunting. Then there are the demands of family: chores, responsibilities, taking care of a younger sibling. And there are the social demands (which can be fun, of course, but take time), like getting together with friends or talking on the phone to a friend who needs your comfort or advice. Then you have to have personal time to eat, sleep, shower, and (hopefully) relax, too.

So, the life of a teenager is actually quite stressful. Here's one stress reducer that is easy to do. It is called "progressive relaxation." Start by getting into a comfortable position, like lying on your bed or sitting in an easy chair. Begin by tensing up your toes, keeping the muscles really tight for a couple of seconds, and then letting them relax. Do it a second time, and enjoy the feeling as the muscles relax. Now tighten up your calf muscles. Again, keep the muscles tight for a couple of seconds, and then let them relax. Do this a second time, too. Now your knees. Do the same thing—tensing and relaxing, tensing and relaxing. Now your thighs. Then your butt, your stomach, chest, shoulders, arms, fingers, neck, jaw, face, eyes, forehead, and scalp. Each time, tense up the muscles, relax, and tense/relax again. Remember to focus on the feeling of relaxing, enjoying the warmth and looseness of each muscle group as it relaxes. Let your mind relax along with your body. Be sure to tighten and relax each separate muscle. When you are finished, make sure that every single inch of your body is relaxed. If there are still any tense spots, go back and repeat the exercise for that muscle. Once you are really relaxed, enjoy the feeling for a few minutes before you get going again. The better you learn to cope with stress now, the better off you will be in the future. Because life typically gets more stressful as you get older, the techniques you learn now can help you for years and years to come.

Why do I have mood swings, where one minute I am happy and the next down?
Victoria, age 17

You are not alone in having quick mood swings. Mood swings are normal during adolescence. A study from the University of Chicago found that the moods of some high school students fluctuate every 15 minutes. This usually is caused by the hormonal changes in your body. Also, most teens experience enormous social and academic pressures in high school. Just the thought of those pressures could put you in a bad mood. Your friends probably have gone through, or are going through, the same emotional roller coaster as you are. Talking to friends who understand your emotional roller coaster can help a lot. When you are feeling down, remember that it probably won't last too long.

* * *

Believe it or not, everyone has mood swings, not just teens. Teens, however, do tend to have more mood swings than children or adults. One of the biggest reasons for this is that during the teen years, more than almost any other time in your life, things are changing, inside and out. Your hormones are causing major physical changes, many of which affect your mood. School demands are increasing, parents expect more from you, you need more money to do more things in the outside world, and your circle of friends may be changing. You are supposed to be looking to have more power and control over your life, but you often don't have as much as you need or want. Who wouldn't be moody?

Try not to express your moodiness with people who can't deal with it. Instead, rely on your friends to help you through the rough spots. They know exactly what it is like. You've probably discovered that your friends (who are also going through mood swings) are much more tolerant and understanding of you than your parents. Give it a little time; for most teens, this moodiness evens out as they get older.

What can a teenager do about low self-esteem and low self-confidence?
Francis, age 16

Your question tells me that you are probably struggling with just not feeling very good about yourself and that you are looking for ways to have more positive feelings. One of the best ways to start feeling better is to get involved in something you like to do or would like to accomplish. Remember, you don't have to choose something that is school related, because there are many things outside of school in which your efforts can be rewarded with a feeling of accomplishment. It might be working, volunteering, raising an animal, growing a garden, helping other family members, performing music, or making art—there are so many choices. Accomplishments make us feel good. But remember, it is important that whatever you choose, it must be something that *you* are interested in or care about, not something that someone else expects of you or you think you *should* do. Too many times negative feelings are the result of trying to fulfill the dreams of another rather than actually fulfilling your own.

* * *

Not feeling very good about yourself happens to most teenage girls at some point during their adolescent years. Whether it is being unhappy about your weight, your complexion, your friends, or your relationship with your parents, during the teen years there always seems to be something that you really wish you could change. If too many of these feelings happen at the same time, or too many problems come up all at once, it can feel so overwhelming that it is difficult to bounce back. Eventually, your self-esteem begins to suffer, and you lose confidence in yourself as a person. This damage can even be long-lasting. So, what can you do to protect your self-esteem?

Try this. Take a bunch of index cards and on each one, write down something that you like about yourself or something good in your life. You can ask your friends to fill out some cards for you, too. Ask them to list all your good points. When you are done, you will have your own "self-esteem deck of cards." Each week, try to add at least one card to your deck. Encourage one or more of your friends to try this with you. Then you can support each other by sharing your decks of cards. Writing down positive things about yourself and saying them out loud is sure to boost your self-esteem and self-confidence.

How do I get more drive to do things (homework, sports, activities)?
Morgan, age 17

You asked a tough question! Here's the deal on drive: You are at an age and stage in your development in which your drive (motivation) has to come from within. Prior to this time, you could do work and get involved in activities because it would please your parents or other important people in your life. As you grow older, however, "sustained motivation," which is motivation that lasts more than a short time, has to come from the personal satisfaction *you* get from doing the work or activity.

This can get a little complicated though, because there are two parts you need to consider. Motivation and performance are like two riders on a tandem bicycle. The first rider is performance. Some people measure their worth *only* by their performance. How well they perform becomes a measure of their value as a person. If you define your worth only by your performance though, you're in trouble, because there are always variables that you can't control—things that come between what you aim for and what you get as an outcome. This is as true in schoolwork as it is in sports. We cannot always control the outcomes.

But the other rider on the bike—motivation—believes that it is the amount of effort that is the most important thing. This rider knows when she's pedaling hard or just coasting along. How hard you pedal is something you can control. You know when you're putting in maximum effort and when you're blowing something off. Our sense of value or worth comes from the good feelings that result from putting in lots of effort.

So, if you want to get more drive to do things, focus on motivation (your effort), not performance (the outcome). This means that the effort you put in is what makes you feel good. The end result, performance, comes second. While effort doesn't always equal outcome, it almost always makes a big difference and says a lot about who you are as a person. Finally, remember that doing your best means doing the best you can given the circumstances. Your best will vary because the pressures in your life will vary from day to day.

* * *

It might be helpful to think about why it's hard for you to get the drive to do things. Are you not getting enough rest, are you stressed or under a lot of pressure, are you not doing things that are fun for you, or are you feeling sad? All of these things can make you feel like you don't have a lot of drive. It's also really important to get enough sleep and eat well to have the energy to get through the day. The pressures of trying to balance school, a job, spending time with friends and family, or other activities can also make you feel tired. You might need help organizing things or need to cut back on some things a little bit. Sometimes people feel like they don't have drive to do something because the activity doesn't really interest them. There are usually some things that might not always be fun that you do have to do (like homework). It often helps to make a list of things you need to do and put those tasks that are hardest at the top of this list. This way, you get them out of the way, feel good that you accomplished them, and then get to move on to things that you enjoy more. Other times there are things that you do have some choice about. For example, if you find that you don't like volleyball and instead want to try basketball, think about making a change. Making choices where you *can* will help you get the motivation to do those things that you *must* do.

I tend to have a problem with controlling my temper. I often blow up very easily, and once I start, I can't stop. How can I learn to control this? *Hilda, age 17*

By acknowledging your need to control your anger you have taken the first step toward change, and you should congratulate yourself. Now, think about what makes you so angry. Does your out-of-control anger get going when you are with a certain person? Does it happen if you don't think you are being heard or when you think a situation is unfair? Do you feel pressures you can't control, so you take your frustrations out on everyone? Try keeping a diary and write down when and how often you feel this intense anger. When you figure out what touches off your anger, then you can begin to get hold of it. Try walking away from the situations (or friends) that trigger this reaction. This will give you a time-out to think through your feelings. If you think your anger is justified, ask yourself if simply being mad will resolve the problem. Then think about how you can express your anger in a way that will help to solve the problem rather than cause more pain to yourself and others.

While raging anger may feel good at the moment, it usually does not lead to understanding. Try to express your own feelings ("I felt hurt when everyone went to the game and didn't tell me") rather than lashing out at others. If you like to write, put your anger down on paper. It's a great way to get your feelings out. If you still feel the need to lash out, get yourself a punching bag, go for a run, channel your negative energy into a positive force.

* * *

It's really good that you recognize that you have a problem controlling your temper. It shows that you want to learn to be responsible in expressing your feelings. First, you need to know that it's always OK *to feel angry*. But what often gets teens in trouble is how they *express their anger* (yelling, swearing, hitting, saying disrespectful things). Sometimes when people get really angry, it's hard for them to think straight, and they may say or do things they ordinarily wouldn't. If you find that you blow up when you get angry, you need to know that there are options in terms of how you can behave differently.

First, you need to learn to recognize the signs when you first start to get angry (like feeling warm, muscles tensing, or heart starting to pound) or know what really triggers you (like a confrontation about a particular subject or with a certain person). When these signs first appear, you can try saying things to yourself like "I can handle this situation," "Stay calm," or "I'm not going to let this get to me." You can also try taking deep breaths to relax your body or counting slowly to 10 before speaking again. Humor can also be a good way to reduce and release some of the tension that goes along with feeling angry. Some people find it helpful to have a brief time-out period to cool down or temporarily leave the situation (take a walk, listen to music, write in a journal) and then come back to finish the discussion when they feel more in control.

How can I work on being more talkative and comfortable with strangers? *Dierdre, age 18*

Being uncomfortable around new people is natural and expected. Part of our training as children is to learn who is safe and who is unsafe. Your reluctance to approach strangers is an adaptive behavior that you learned to help keep you safe as a child. Now that you are older and want to feel comfortable meeting and interacting with more people outside of your family, the things you learned as a child can get in your way, and you may see yourself as shy and uneasy. Some people we meet make it easy for us to be comfortable with them right away because of some similarity between ourselves and them. For example, they dress like us, go to the same church, and so on. However, if experiences like this have been rare, you may begin to feel like you are not "good" around strangers and have difficulty getting along with new people.

A good way to begin to feel more comfortable with strangers is to start by practicing introducing yourself to people who you know have a shared interest with you. For example, meeting someone at a dance class may be easier than meeting someone at a party, because you already know that the person in the dance class shares an interest with you. Decide on three places or situations where you are going to take the plunge and introduce yourself to someone new. While at first it will seem very scary, once you see that you can do it, it will get easier and easier.

* * *

Generally people who are shy are secretly telling themselves that they are not as good as the person they are trying to meet. When you do not feel confident, it is natural for you to feel anxious and not want to stick your neck out. One of the ways to begin to feel more confident is to identify what you are thinking and feeling when you meet new people. If you tell yourself that this will be just awful, it is more likely to come out that way. Are you telling yourself that this person is better than you in some way, has more power, looks better, is in control? If so, then you are naturally going to feel inferior and not be able to express the full range of your charm and personality.

What is important to remember is that for every person who is new to you, you are new to her or him as well. It is common to assume that you are the only one feeling nervous and that the other person has no anxiety over meeting someone new. So, it is important to remind yourself that when someone first meets you, she or he is just as likely to have some anxiety as you are. Try some positive self-talk instead of drowning in your negative self-talk. Tell yourself about all the things you have to offer; remind yourself of all your good qualities. Don't sell yourself short.

You have a great deal to offer, and positive self-talk will help you to feel more confident when speaking with someone new.

* * *

It can be very hard to approach strangers and make conversation. Situations like asking questions at school, making small talk at a party, or asking for a raise at work make many people nervous. It's great that you want to work on being more comfortable with people, and confronting your uncomfortable feelings is exactly what you need to do to overcome them. First, think about what situations make you nervous, self-conscious, or uncomfortable. You can even make a list if you want. Then "practice" talking with people you know and trust. Pretend that you are in a situation that would usually make you uncomfortable, and practice what you would say. You can also think about topics to use in conversations with people you would like to be able to talk with. What do you know about them? Do they like music or movies? Are they in a class with you? Thinking of topics ahead of time will help you feel more secure, like when you prepare for a test.

After you've practiced and prepared yourself, try it out for real. Pick one person you want to be more comfortable with and set a goal for yourself, like "I'm going to say hello tomorrow." Or decide on a question you'll ask this person or a comment you'll make. Then, you can work on trying to have longer conversations. Go as slowly as you need to. Remember, learning to be comfortable with strangers is like learning to swim in the shallow end of the pool and then gradually moving to the deep end.

Why are girls always expected to be so calm and gentle? *Janice, age 12*

It does seem like forever that girls have been expected to be calm, quiet, and "nice." In fact, there is an old saying that you may not have heard of, but your grandmother might know, that girls are made of "sugar and spice and everything nice." While treating others with courtesy and respect is important, it is equally important that girls speak up and say what they think and how they feel. If you don't feel comfortable or know how to do this, practice with a friend, a parent, a teacher, or a friend's mother. Ask them how they voice their thoughts and feelings, particularly those that others may not agree with. By the way, this is equally important for boys. Boys need to learn to speak their feelings and not just act like "snakes and snails and puppy dog tails."

* * *

Every culture has images for how boys and girls, men and women, should behave. In our society, boys are expected to be strong, rational, independent, and somewhat tough. They are not supposed to show too much "softness," fear, sadness, or uncertainty. In contrast, girls are supposed to be attentive to the needs of others, caring, interested in relationships, and not express anger. These expectations make it hard for adolescent girls to behave in ways that are authentic and real. For example, if you get angry and you've been taught that girls are not supposed to get angry, you'll feel some conflict. It is important that you do not try to pretend that you're not angry, and it is equally important that you do not express your anger in ways that will make you feel bad about yourself.

While you are certainly not going to be calm and gentle when you are feeling mad, you can clearly and assertively state that you are angry. This is not disrespectful, even though the person may not like hearing that you are angry. Being calm and gentle all the time is not only unrealistic, it's not healthy.

* * *

In most cultures, males and females are expected to behave differently and have different roles. Some experts believe that these expectations are caused by biological differences between men and women. For example, because females have the hormones that allow them to bear children, they also have become the primary caretakers of children. For this reason, females learned the role of being nurturing and caring of others (being calm and gentle). In contrast, male hormones have been suggested as a reason for boys being more active and aggressive than girls. Boys also have a larger bone structure than girls, which allows them to be involved in more activities that require physical endurance and strength. Therefore, parents often teach their sons to be strong, dominant, and competitive to prepare them for their future roles as providers and protectors of the family. Parents often teach their girls to be warm, calm, and gentle to prepare them for their future roles as mothers.

You can see this clearly if you look at the different kinds of toys, games, and extracurricular activities for girls compared with those for boys. Girls traditionally play with dolls and tea sets and they take dance lessons, while boys play with trucks and action figures and prefer contact sports. Even TV, magazines, and video games reinforce these ideas about how girls and boys are supposed to act. In spite of the women's rights movement, our society continues to promote these traditional stereotypes. So, you're going to have to work hard to pay attention to your own voice in spite of others' expectations. This may mean being calm and gentle sometimes, but on other occasions, you'll need to be able to be strong and assertive.

Is it true that girls mature faster than boys? If so, why? *Roslyn, age 15*

Girls do mature faster than boys. The physical changes associated with adolescence usually occur earlier for girls than for boys. During early adolescence, girls are often taller than boys, and many of the physical changes, like developing breasts, make them begin to look more like adults. In fact, because of this, parents, teachers, and others often expect more grown-up behavior from adolescent girls than from boys (while at the same time, they often give the boys more freedom, like later curfews).

Changes in behavior often go along with the physical changes. The person they see in the mirror looks more like an adult, so they try to match the way they act with this more mature image. So for a time, particularly during early adolescence, there is often a gap between boys and girls. This gap starts to close during the first years of high school, when the boys catch up physically. So, even though you are now a foot taller than Steve, and he acts like such a baby, it doesn't mean that in a few years he won't be the guy that all the girls dream about.

* * *

It is true that most girls mature faster than most boys. If you remember, beginning in about the fifth or sixth grade, most girls got taller and developed physically faster than most boys. This is a biological fact. It is also true that most girls become interested in boys at an earlier age than boys become interested in girls. Many girls between ages 12 and 14 find it very frustrating that boys their age act so "stupid." Often it isn't until high school that the changes begin to even out. This might be one of the reasons why, traditionally, girls are interested in older guys and often eventually marry men who are at least a few years older than they are.

Why are girls more sensitive than guys?
Zoe, age 13

You know, it often seems like girls are more emotionally sensitive than guys, especially teenage guys. We don't know all the reasons, but we have some ideas about why this appears to be true. Once a girl reaches 12 or so and begins to mature physically, it seems as though nature is preparing her to be sensitive to others the way a mother might be to her baby, to feel what others feel so she can provide love and support to her children. Our culture tells boys different things. They are expected to be "tough" and not get carried away by their feelings. In ancient days, men were hunters, and women stayed with the children. The men had to pay attention to finding food and protecting the village. They couldn't afford to get too emotionally upset and lose their concentration. Boys probably have more aggressive instincts for this reason.

These days we don't have to hunt for food much, and most of us don't live in small villages prone to attack. But the physical differences between males and females are still there, and over the years, girls and boys have gotten used to playing different roles. In addition, the two sexes have different hormones in their bodies that seem to affect how sensitive they are.

In spite of all this, don't think that girls cannot be assertive and that boys cannot be sensitive. In fact, boys do feel emotions, but many of them simply don't know how to express their feelings or fear that they will be teased. You might be surprised at how sensitive some boys are if you simply ask them about how they feel.

* * *

Teen girls spend a lot more time than guys thinking and talking together about what is going on, especially about relationships with each other and with boys. At the same time, guys discover that they may have more privileges, such as more freedom to go where they please. They are more interested in new possibilities for activities than in talking with each other. This leads guys to be more "action oriented" and less concerned with how others think and feel. Girls, on the other hand, learn to perfect their skills in being sensitive to their friends. Therefore, it is not surprising that girls and women in general come across as being more sensitive.

Are girls supposed to do better than boys, or do we just put too much pressure on ourselves? *Anna, age 12*

Some girls, especially young teens, feel that their parents and teachers expect them to do better than boys in school. Is it "supposed" to be this way? Probably not, but the pressure can feel very real, and the challenge is to learn to cope with the pressure. To begin with, it helps to think about who you are, what

22

your goals are, and how they fit together. This is part of forming your own identity. And feeling good about yourself and your choices is your most powerful weapon in keeping the pressure from boiling over.

Feeling good in these ways is called "self-esteem" or "positive self-regard." All of us have special talents and skills, some that we are born with and some that we learn as we grow up. And all of us have weaknesses too, things that we cannot do as well as we would like. For example, I can't sing even though I would love to be able to carry a tune. As you grow and develop, learning to accept your strengths (talents) and your limitations is one of the most helpful ways of reducing pressure.

It is damaging to think that having limitations equals being inferior. It is important to realize that your limitations do not make you inferior. They simply mean that you are human, in other words, not perfect. So pay attention to your strengths, and work to accept your limitations. This may sound easy, but actually it can be hard to do. But think for a moment. If you really took pride in the things that you do well, what would your life be like? What would you think of yourself? Now, if you focus on your limitations, how do you feel about yourself? By looking at the difference between these two feelings, you can begin to reduce the pressure by appreciating your unique strengths and talents.

* * *

Whether girls are supposed to do better than boys or not, many of them feel they should. This is like falling into a "pressure trap" that's hard to get out of. Constantly comparing yourself with others can make you feel miserable, filled with tension and anxiety. One of the ways to prevent yourself from falling into this trap is to take a close look at *your own strengths and weaknesses* and *your own goals.* You might begin by making a list of the things that are important to you that you can do well. Include not only school subjects but also other talents that you have, like being a good listener, being good with animals, or even being a good artist or a computer whiz. Now make a list of things that you *wish* you were good at but that you have come to realize are not your greatest strengths. Look at the list of the things you wish you were better at and think about how much pressure you put on yourself to be someone you might not be. While it is certainly fine to work hard to develop a skill or to become good at something, it is equally important to accept that you have some limitations, and so, in spite of trying your hardest, you may not be able to be at the top. Now look at your list of things you do well. Take pride in your talents and accomplishments. Adolescent girls often don't pay attention to their strengths but instead only focus on their weaknesses. Learning to focus on your strengths will not only reduce the pressure but will also bring you positive self-esteem.

Hot Tips

☞ No one is good at everything—pay attention to your strengths. If you've done your best, learn to accept your limitations.

☞ You're not imagining it—most teen girls are "older" than teen boys. Girls mature faster, physically and emotionally.

☞ Want to improve your self-esteem and confidence? Pursue stuff you like to do. Motivation is a key to success.

☞ Sensitivity does not equal silence. Give "voice" to your thoughts and feelings. Practice your assertiveness skills.

☞ Measure your success by *your effort*, not *your performance*. While you can't always control the outcome, you can control your input.

☞ There is nothing wrong with *feeling* angry. It's how you *express* your anger that can cause big problems. Learn what "triggers" your anger, and practice effective ways to express your feelings.

☞ Your mood swings are *normal*, but your parents might not understand. Try to keep your cool around them.

☞ Feel stressed? Plan ahead and watch out for "unrealistic" expectations of yourself. Sometimes you simply have to *let something go.*

2

What's Happening to My Body?

I'm always worried about how I look—my hair, my weight, my complexion. I want to have a certain image, but I can't seem to look exactly the way I want to. Sometimes I look so fat, even though my friends tell me I look fine. I really don't understand why my body keeps changing so much. I don't even really feel like *me*. I've got so many questions about what is happening to me, but I'm too embarrassed to ask anyone. I wish I knew more about sex and stuff.
—*Amy*

Why are teenagers so worried about their image? Why is image everything in this society? *Tess, age 17*

Teenagers worry about their "image" because during the teen years, more than at any other time, your image is used by your peers to make many assumptions about what you are like as a person. Therefore, how you are seen can affect whether or not you are included in certain groups, invited to certain parties and events, or included in lunch table conversations. Adults also seem to make assumptions about teens based on how they look. Some parents will not want their kids to hang out with other teens who look a certain way, even though they don't know them at all. In many ways, using someone's appearance as a determining factor in deciding what a person is like is a cop-out—it's an easy way to not spend the time required to really know who an individual is. Although how you look does not communicate all of who you are, you do have some choices. Even if you don't like the fact that people make assumptions about you on the basis of your appearance, you do have some control over how you look. So, you can, if you choose to, take some control over how you use your image to communicate something about who you are.

* * *

Part of growing up is forming an identity. As you become an adult, you learn more of who you are (your identity), and in order to be a healthy and happy adult, you have to be comfortable with your identity. But identity has two parts: an inner part and an outer part. Your inner identity is what you believe about yourself, whether you think you are smart or dumb, whether you think you are attractive or ugly, whether you believe you are especially talented or athletic or just average. But the other part of your identity is the outer part—how you fit in, how you seem to others, what others think of you, the group you hang out with. We don't exist in a vacuum, so the reality is that this outer part of your identity, your *image*, is part of how you define yourself. In our society, sometimes we are led to believe that image is everything, but you should never forget the inner part of your identity, who you are inside. While your image is one way you communicate who you are, it is only your shell, not your heart and soul.

Why are most females not pleased about the way they look? *Susan, age 15*

Unfortunately, in today's society, most girls are unhappy with at least one major part of how they look. And in your teenage years, there is a lot of focus on looks. Magazines, TV, and movies all present images of girls that are impossible for the average teen to reach. This leaves girls feeling that how they look is never quite good enough and makes some teenage girls very critical of themselves and each other. It is important that girls fight against these stereotypes and learn to appreciate and enjoy their own unique look. One idea of something that you and your friends can do together is to create your own expert advice column to help teen girls fight against the way the media portrays how women "should" look. In it, you can focus on how important it is for girls to enjoy those things about their bodies that the media often makes them feel bad about.

If you are from an African American or Hispanic culture, you probably have a different view of what makes your body beautiful than White teens. Studies have shown that African American and Latina girls often have a healthier (and more realistic) body image than White girls. For example, what a White girl would consider to be a butt that is too big or boobs that are too large would be thought of as the perfect size by a girl from a different culture. So, in the end, loving your body means not buying into the media image. Instead, expand your definition of what makes for a beautiful woman's body.

* * *

Sometimes the dissatisfaction with how you look on the outside is really about not liking yourself on the *inside*. So how can you begin to have more positive feelings about yourself? It definitely helps to find something you like to do and then to do that thing to the best of your ability. This doesn't have to be something academic, because there are tons of things outside of school where your effort can be rewarded with a feeling of accomplishment. It might be taking a job, volunteering, raising an animal, growing a garden, helping other family members, performing music, or making art—there are endless choices. What is most important is that you choose something that excites you. Too many times negative feelings about yourself are the result of trying to fulfill the dreams of others, rather than actually fulfilling your own.

Why am I always so concerned about how much I weigh? *Gina, age 13*

During adolescence, a lot of girls become concerned about their weight because our society emphasizes looks rather than personality or character. Most girls do not realize that practically all girls gain weight during puberty. This weight gain is part of normal female development. If you walk through an art museum and look at the statues of women, you can appreciate that women's bodies are meant to be filled with "hills and valleys," as one girl described it. A woman's body is art and is beautiful. Although it is natural to be concerned about your appearance, realize that your concern is heightened by magazines and TV programs that feature girls and women whose bodies are not at all typical of most normal people. Your body is your own and unique, not like your mother's, your sister's, your aunt's, or your friend's. The best way to take care of your body is to eat healthy foods and exercise in some way, like walking, biking, or whatever appeals to you. Your personality is what is most important, and it will shine through your body, whatever its size or shape.

Why do people say they're fat, when they really aren't? *Eva, age 14*

Many girls who say they're fat really believe that they *are* fat. These girls don't always see themselves as others see them, just as you may not see yourself as others do. Try not to get mad at them or accuse them of just trying to get attention. Instead, notice something about them that looks good. If you have a friend who thinks she's fat (and really isn't), try to stay out of arguments and debates about her weight. Instead, try to compliment her about her hair or clothes or about one of her accomplishments. This is one of the ways to help girls who are too focused on their weight to pay attention to their strengths.

And do yourself the same favor! Keep a list of the things you like about yourself. Make sure to compliment yourself at least once a day. It can really help on those days when you simply hate the way you look.

Are people born gay, do they acquire it over a period of time, or both? *Greta, age 16*

Your question is one that has been the subject of numerous studies and articles over the past two decades. As yet, no one has come up with a definitive answer. However, there appears to be mounting evidence that homosexuality is influenced by both nature (people are born with a preference for same-sex sexual partners) and nurture (the preference for same-sex partners is at least partially determined by experiences growing up). Some researchers believe they have discovered actual biological differences between some heterosexual and homosexual men, but these differences do not show up all the time. What's most important, however, is that we accept and respect each person's right to her or his own sexual preference.

Unfortunately, while our society has become more accepting of gay rights, we still have a long way to go. Many gay individuals continue to be rejected by friends and family and discriminated against by employers. You can help end this kind of discrimination by educating yourself and others about the need for all of us to accept and respect gay individuals.

* * *

Like most things in nature, there are complicated mechanisms at work. Sexual identity, whether it is heterosexual, gay, or bisexual, comes from many influences. Most doctors and scientists believe that the way we form our sexual identity is a combination of factors, including biology, learning, and environment. Many researchers believe that there is a large biological component to sexual identity, so that people are "born" gay—and many gay men and lesbians agree that they have known they were gay from a very young age. But some gay men and women feel that their sexual identity is their choice: not something they are born with but something they have decided

on. Even if biology is a main factor, though, how people behave and express themselves sexually has a lot
to do with learning, psychology, and culture.

When should I start shaving? When is the right time to start wearing a bra? *Elise, age 12*

The time to start shaving or to start wearing a bra
differs for every girl. It all depends on how your body
is growing and changing. For shaving, it also depends
on whether you choose to shave at all. Some girls and
women don't feel that it is necessary to shave their
legs and underarms. However, if you do feel that you
would like to shave, you should start when you feel
you have enough hair—a short stubble. If you don't
have enough hair, it might hurt or you might feel a
slight burning sensation when you shave. Talking
about this with your mother, aunt, or older sister, or
even your school nurse, can also be helpful.

In the same way, there is no right time to start
wearing a bra. When I was growing up, my pediatrician told me to try this test: Put a pencil under your
breast, and let go of the pencil. If your breast hangs
over the pencil enough to keep it from falling you
should be wearing a bra; otherwise it's up to you. Remember, it's your body, and these kinds of decisions
are yours to make.

* * *

Both of these questions are about special "beginnings" that relate to personal choices and needs

among girls. They also signify milestones on the path to womanhood. Deciding the right time to shave or wear a bra usually involves a parent and is an easier decision to make when both a parent and daughter are ready for these big steps around the same time. Most girls start shaving and wearing bras in middle school, but in some cases, family values or later physical development might postpone making these choices until high school.

One of the things almost all young girls are told about shaving is that once you start you must shave regularly, because a few days' growth of leg hair can be considered unattractive. Obviously, this is a matter of taste, and you can always let leg hair grow back to its original, natural state. Some parents encourage their daughters to delay shaving underarm hair until the odor that comes with puberty creates more of a need. So why rush it? Because shaving is a rite of passage and a signal of membership in one's peer group, sometimes girls want to start shaving despite a parent's urge to delay.

Wanting to start to wear a bra can also be based on the need to belong to your peer group. When girls are slow to develop, wearing a sports or training bra —which requires no beginning signs of puberty whatsoever—can help you feel much less self-conscious with your faster developing friends. If this is true for you, you may need to talk to your parents directly about your feelings, because a generation ago women usually started wearing bras only based on need. On the other extreme, some girls experience breast development as early as third or fourth grade and feel very self-conscious about it. When this happens, sometimes a parent (or even a friend or pediatrician) might encourage you to wear a bra before you are comfortable.

You and your parent may not be ready for these beginnings at the same time. That is why communication is so important. Girls need to tell their parents how they feel about these issues and what the issues mean to them personally.

What will I do when I get my period? Should I tell anyone when I do get it?
Katelyn, age 12

Each young woman has her own way of responding to this event. Getting your period might be a big deal; it may be scary, exciting, embarrassing—or no big deal at all. There's no right or wrong way to feel, no one you have to tell. What you do and who you tell depend on how comfortable you feel and how much you already know about getting your period. You certainly don't *have* to tell anyone if you don't feel comfortable talking about it.

However, you don't have to feel uncomfortable about bringing up this issue, as this is something that all women go through. In fact, it is very common for a girl to tell her mother, an aunt, or an older sister when she gets her period. Not only might your mother or relative be interested to know that you are maturing, she may also be able to offer advice about caring for yourself when you have your period, like about wearing pads or tampons, and can answer any questions that you may have. As for telling a friend, again, you don't have to if you don't feel comfortable sharing this with her. However, you and your friend might enjoy exchanging your experiences and feelings about this passage into womanhood.

* * *

The most important part about getting your period is feeling prepared. This means that you have an understanding about how menstruation works and the supplies you will need when you start your period. Understanding what is happening to your body will help you be emotionally ready for your period. If you are prepared, then you can handle your period the way you handle the rest of your hygiene, like shampooing your hair or brushing your teeth. It takes time, some planning ahead, and some responsibility, but most teen girls would agree that it is just one of those tasks that you get good at with a little practice.

Before you start your period, you really don't know if you are going to have a heavy or a light flow, so it is common to be kind of nervous about it and need to go to the bathroom a lot to check things out. The first few periods are usually light, and this helps girls get comfortable with the whole procedure. When you have some breast development and pubic and underarm hair growth, you can assume that the time is drawing near for your period to start. This is a good time to start carrying supplies like pads or tampons. Just keep them in a discreet zippered pouch in your purse or school bag, and then you don't have to worry about being taken by surprise. Don't forget—you are not alone with your concern. Many adults have no idea how many girls worry about your exact question!

Girls' comfort levels in talking about their periods vary a lot. There is no reason you have to tell anyone about when you start your period, but because it is a significant event in your life, it can feel good to share the news with someone you trust. Lots of girls will want to share it with their mothers and their best friends, but there will always be those who are very private by nature and will want to keep it to themselves. Hopefully, all girls have had a chance to talk to friends and adults about menstruation at some point so that they feel fully informed, comfortable with the whole process, and supported for their feelings about it. The important thing is to not feel alone. If you want some support or help, take the leap and find someone to talk to. Even though it might feel awkward to talk about it, it is sometimes remarkable how good it can feel to share the news because it usually results in an outpouring of support, reassurance, and warmth. After all, it is the beginning of womanhood, and others enjoy welcoming you to the clan.

Why do people joke about your period?
Darcy, age 13

Some girls joke about their periods because periods are a new experience for them, and they may feel embarrassed. Other people joke, boys in particular, because they don't understand periods, and they feel awkward and embarrassed, too. Sometimes boys try to embarrass girls by saying things like, "Oh, she's PMSing, no wonder she is acting that way." Remember, when they say such dumb things, it is usually an excuse for something they don't understand about a girl. It can help to talk with older girls who have managed to live through those comments and who feel good about themselves. As you get older and grow more confident and comfortable with yourself and your body, you probably will not be bothered by references to periods.

Hot Tips

☞ Thinking about shaving or wearing a bra? Talk to a trusted friend, older sister, even your parents. Then decide what *you* want to do.

☞ Getting your period is a celebration of your femininity! Although there is no rule that says you have to tell anyone, most girls feel better when they talk to someone they trust.

☞ *Don't* measure your attractiveness by the women you see on TV and in magazines. *Normal* women don't look like them.

☞   What's on the inside is much more important than your size or shape.

☞   There is nothing wrong or crazy about being gay. Being gay is *totally normal*.

☞   Your body is your castle. Treat it with great care, and it will pay off for the rest of your life.

☞   Like it or not, how you look influences how others see you. Pay attention to what you want to *say* about yourself.

☞   There are some things you can't change about your looks. But you can enhance your appearance by eating right, exercising, and staying healthy.

3

Girlfriends and Boyfriends—Why Is It All So Complicated?

My social life is a mess. Some of the girls in school are really mean to me, even though they hardly know me. Then there is this guy that I like a lot, but I have no idea if he even knows I exist. I'm not sure if I'm ready to have a boyfriend anyway. Some of my friends who have boyfriends don't seem so happy either—it seems like they are always fighting. Then there's my "friend" Lisa who is totally boy crazy. The last two times we were going to hang out she ditched me to be with him. I really don't know what to do about any of this stuff.
—Bethany

How can I make guy friends? *Ingrid, age 13*

All people, particularly guys, like to talk about themselves. One of the easiest ways to get to know a guy is to ask him questions. They don't have to be complex questions. You could ask him, "What did you think of that test today?" or ask him about some sport he is interested in. Ask questions that are not answered by just "yes" or "no," because then the conversation stops. Through conversing, you can discover if he is the type of guy you would like to get to know better.

And, in case no one has told you, boys often don't like to make eye contact, so if he doesn't look at you directly, don't jump to the conclusion that you are being rejected. Some boys feel awkward with a girl and may not know how to go about talking with you. You can make it easier for them by trying to open up a conversation about something they know about or are familiar with. Asking about school activities is an easy way to start. Then you can move on to explore other areas, like TV shows, movies, or sports.

* * *

One of the best ways to make guy friends is to get involved in activities with them. Because most school sports teams are divided into guys and girls, you have to look in other places. Some of the activities that guys often get involved with are school radio and TV stations, debate clubs, ski clubs, and also playing pool, Ping-Pong, or video games. Meeting guy friends this way is almost always a lot easier than just trying to strike up a conversation in class or in the hall. Sharing activities and interests naturally leads to conversation, which then leads to friendship. And just think—meeting guys this way will get you to try some things you probably never would have tried.

Is it appropriate for a girl to ask a boy out? *Carol, age 12*

While society still tends to see the male as the "leader" in pursuing the female, your question is a good one. You probably don't realize just how many other girls have the same question. And it is really great that you are thinking ahead about situations you might encounter when you are ready to date. Times have changed, and girls are increasingly more assertive in pursuing what they want. When you start dating, if you are thinking about asking a boy out, go for it! While your friends might tease you a little, they'll be happy that you did it because it will make it easier for them to do it when they want to.

It's important to remember that boys can be nervous, too. They often feel just as scared about asking a girl out. The boy might be interested in you but is too shy to ask. If you ask, he might say yes. If he says no, it'll hurt for a while. But you'll get over it. Everyone does. And nobody gets through life without being rejected sometimes.

* * *

When you are old enough to date, it is certainly OK to ask a boy out if you want to. Just like some girls, a boy can be shy or afraid of rejection. Think about how you might feel when you want to be asked out. Some boys will feel the same way. No matter how old you are, if there is a guy you are interested in, it's easier to start with a friendship. Many romances start as friendships, so later on your friendship can become something more. Instead of going out just the two of you, try getting together with him in a small group of friends. Hang out with him, and see if you really like him.

Some girls think they are being too forward or "aggressive" if they ask a boy out, but this is more a question of your style. More and more, it is common practice for anyone to ask anyone else out regardless of whether it is the boy or the girl asking. It can be a sign of maturity that you know what you like and are willing to ask for it. Some boys feel flattered when asked out. And then, of course, there are those old-fashioned guys who just won't like it. But those guys are probably not right for you anyway.

What makes a good boyfriend? *Yolanda, age 13*

You've really asked a great question. I bet many women wished they knew to ask this question at your age. A good boyfriend respects you as an equal. He shows his respect by being interested in what you say. And he treats you the same when his friends are around as when he's with you alone.

You can trust him to do what he says, like call you if he says he'll call. He makes you feel good about yourself—all of you, how smart you are, what you look like, the things you like to do. He doesn't pressure you for sex or cheat on you. He never physically hurts you and, if he hurts your feelings, he says he's sorry and really works hard never to do it again.

* * *

A good boyfriend demonstrates the kind of values that are important to you, like genuineness, honesty, and loyalty (he doesn't go out with other girls behind your back). The way your boyfriend treats you is *very* important. Can you and your boyfriend communicate? Can you share feelings about important things with him? Do you trust him not to tell other people secrets you may have shared with him? Does he share his thoughts and feelings with you? A good boyfriend should be sensitive to your feelings and understanding of you.

Can you be yourself around your boyfriend, or do you feel that you are always putting on a show for him? Being able to be relaxed and natural with your boyfriend means that there is a lot of mutual acceptance between the two of you. Does your boyfriend show you affection in ways that you like, such as holding your hand or putting his arm around you? A good boyfriend will treat you as an equal and respect your wishes about important matters. He will understand the word "no," especially about sex. He will also be OK when you want to spend time with your family or friends. A good boyfriend won't smother you and demand all of your time.

Another "must" is a good sense of humor. Does your boyfriend make you laugh, and do you have fun with him? Boyfriends are more fun if they share similar interests and like to do some of the things you like to do. Remember, in choosing a boyfriend, there are a lot of great guys out there, so don't settle for less than you want and deserve.

Why are some girls "boy crazy"? *Margot, age 18*

It's more than OK to like boys and to want to have a boyfriend—most girls do. "Boy crazy," though, means that a girl is overly concerned about meeting boys and getting a boyfriend. Having a boyfriend is more important to her than anything else. She is preoccupied with boy watching and boys' opinions to the exclusion of everything else.

Some girls are boy crazy because they need a lot of attention and aren't getting it from home, especially from their fathers. Others need boys to provide some of the qualities they need and want but think they can't get for themselves, like power (he will protect her all the time) or status (thinking people will admire her because of who her boyfriend is) or independence (he has a car and can give her a ride somewhere or an excuse to get out of her house for awhile). Girls who are boy crazy often have not developed their own identity and don't have a life of their own. Unfortunately, these girls don't invest their time in finding out who *they* are and don't develop their own abilities and interests. Instead, they give up their own development for the pursuit of boys. Sadly, girls who are boy crazy just don't think they are as important as having a boyfriend is.

If you have a friend who is boy crazy, try talking to her. Or even show her this book. It might get her thinking.

* * *

There's lots of pressure to hook up with a guy. There's a hidden message in our society that a girl is not OK if she is not interested in a relationship with a guy. In fact, for most teenage girls, having a boy-friend really boosts their self-confidence. But having a boyfriend shouldn't be the only way to feel happy and secure. Girls who are boy crazy are driven to have a boyfriend as if their lives depended on it. They forget about finding other ways to make themselves feel important and valuable, and they often lose out on developing their interests, talents, and friendships with other girls. Being boy crazy means you're missing out on too many other things. It's like having a one-track mind. You can't see anything else, even yourself.

What should I do if my boyfriend tells me to pick between him and my friends?
Juanita, age 13

The first thing to do is to find out why he feels that way. Ask him—or ask his friends if he won't say.

Maybe your boyfriend doesn't like your friends. His reason for not liking your friends might be something that seems obvious to him but that you never thought of. Maybe you'll be able to do something about it. For example, maybe your friends tease him, and you could ask them to stop. Maybe you'll find out that he's jealous of the time that you spend with your friends, and you could balance your time better. Maybe knowing his reason will make you decide that he's not for you —say, if what he really wants is to control your life by taking up all of your time.

The second thing to do is to find out how strongly he feels about this issue. Sometimes people feel strongly about something at one moment and say things that they don't really mean. For example, he might be mad about something that will pass, or he might just be tired and irritable. Some problems do just go away if you give them a little time.

Finally, if your boyfriend really pushes, think about what your life will be like without him. Compare that with what your life will be like without your friends. Do you want to give up all your friendships? Most girls don't. You need to ask yourself whether you want him to be your whole life. And think about what else you can do (like get another guy). It's your choice.

* * *

Dump him! Dump him! Dump him! He's foolish, immature, and selfish. Who needs him? And don't be surprised if he comes running back, willing to share you with your friends. And then think long and hard about whether or not you really want to share your time with him.

Why are guy friends always so two-faced? Why do they act different when they are with their guy friends than with their girl friends? *Eunice, age 17*

It's not only teenage guys who seem to change their behavior when their friends are around. Guys say the same thing about girls. They want to know why you act differently when your friends are around, too! But let's focus on your question first. During their teen years, guys are trying to establish their identity as men. In our culture, becoming a man has many stereotypes associated with it, especially ones that say that a "real man" is physically and emotionally strong. Guys are not supposed to cry or look for emotional support or help. They are supposed to be able to solve their problems themselves.

Of course, just like girls, guys have lots of feelings and, during their teen years, have lots of the same struggles as girls do. The big difference is that in our culture girls are given the message that it is OK to be emotional and talk about their problems. So, when guys are with their girl friends they don't have to pretend as much. They can "let down" a little and not have to worry that other guys are thinking they are not real men. When they are back with their guy friends, they often feel a need to hide the emotional parts of themselves so they don't get laughed at.

If you really think about it, many girls also change their behavior when they are with their male friends. During the teen years, guys and girls both behave somewhat differently when they are with their same-sex friends compared with when they are with their opposite-sex friends. However, things are slowly changing for guys as the message gets out that it is OK and healthy for them to let down their guard and show their emotions, even when they are with their guy friends!

* * *

Most people will admit that they act differently to some degree with different people. I'll bet when you are with your parents you act differently than when you are with your friends! I'll bet, too, that you act differently with your close friends than with people you hardly know. So guys also could act one way with male friends and another way with girl friends. It's natural to change our behavior in different situations. The problem comes up when someone acts so differently that they come across as a totally different person. That's what makes them seem to be two-faced. What's going on underneath, however, is that he might actually feel differently when he is with his guy friends. Part of becoming more mature is learning more about who you are on the inside, so that you are not so easily influenced by different circumstances.

How do you help a friend get out of an unhealthy relationship when she doesn't believe she's in one? *Darya, age 17*

The truth is, unless people can see that a relationship they are in is "unhealthy," it's almost impossible to get them to leave the relationship. The problem is that we all put on "blinders" when we don't want to face the truth about something, even though we often know, deep down, that something is wrong. In fact, when people have their blinders on they tend to be very, very defensive and "tune out" anything others tell them that they don't want to hear.

Don't stop talking to your friend about your concerns, but realize that it may take her a long time to see "the truth." And, when she finally does see the truth, or the relationship ends for some other reason, don't say "I told you so!" Instead, be supportive and help her see what her experience has taught her about relationships.

* * *

You can try to help, but you can't force your friend to do anything. Part of being a good friend is to be honest: Explain your feelings to your friend, and tell her why you feel the way you do. Tell her exactly what is upsetting to you, what you see in her relationship that is unhealthy. But, remember, you are not responsible for your friend's life, and you are not responsible for making her decisions. You are only responsible for expressing yourself honestly and openly, and then the rest of the responsibility is hers. You can suggest options to her, like giving her support in ending the relationship or seeking professional help from a counselor or psychologist if the relationship is really unhealthy for her. You can assure her that you know that ending the relationship will be really, really, hard but that you will stick by her if she decides to get out of the relationship so she won't feel so lonely. But bottom line is that the decision is hers.

How can you cheer up a friend when she is dumped by a boyfriend? *Claire, age 13*

Much of how we think and feel about ourselves is a function of how others think and feel about us. When others think and feel positively about us, we feel accepted, and this increases our self-esteem and feelings of self-worth ("I am important!"). However, when a friend has been dumped by her boyfriend, the overwhelming feelings may be rejection and low self-worth ("I'm not important").

You can be helpful to your friend by assuring her that you are still her friend, encouraging other friends to show that they care about her, and providing positive words of inspiration to make her feel that she is important and worthwhile as a person. You can also do small things for her, such as making a card to show that you are thinking about her, planning a unique surprise event for her with other friends, and keeping in touch to just talk or listen. The key is to keep her occupied with positive people and positive things. Many broken hearts have been healed with time by the love and care generated by a true friend who gives of herself or himself willingly and unselfishly.

* * *

When people have been hurt, particularly when they have been rejected by someone, they feel terrible. Besides comfort and reassurance, one of the best things you can do for your friend is to get her up and going. Even if she says she's not in the mood, be insistent. Tell her you need her company, that you can't decide which shoes to buy without her, and you don't care if she doesn't even say anything, you just want her to be with you. Get her out to events, parties, or even a movie. Time is a great healer, and even though you may not realize it, keeping your friend active and involved so that time can do its healing is one of the best ways to help her.

Is there a person right for me—you know, love? *Angela, age 16*

If you mean is there only one person in the world who has been created for you, the answer is *no*. A few years ago, there was a popular movie and song called *Somewhere in Time*, which suggested that somewhere in the universe, somewhere in time, either in a past life or in a future life, there would be the perfect match, the perfect love, and the perfect soul mate for each of us. This is simply not true. People change, and the person you may be in love with now and think you want to marry will not be exactly the same 20 years from now.

Look at your parents or your friends' parents; have you seen big changes in any of them? The fantasy that there is only one true love puts more importance on *choosing* the right mate than on being *committed* to working on a relationship. While finding someone you truly love is important, the success of any relationship requires that both people are constantly working on communicating and listening to each other. Finding the right guy does not necessarily mean you will have a great life just because you found him. "Mr. Right" also has to be committed to the idea that relationships require work, and he has to be willing to listen and change as the relationship changes.

So, there is both good news and bad news. The good news is that there are lots and lots of princes out there who are right for you. The bad news is that you have to go through a thousand frogs before you find a single prince. But, don't worry. You have many years to learn how to sort out the frogs from the princes.

* * *

There are probably lots of people who are right for you, but as you mature your definition of "Mr. Right" will change. This happens because between your teen years and adulthood, your needs will change. For example, right now your Mr. Right might be a guy who is good-looking, athletic, popular, and funny. You probably aren't thinking too much about what kind of career he will have, what kind of income he will earn, what kind of father he will be, or even what part of the country he'd want to live in. Right now, these things just don't matter very much, but they will matter later on. Sometimes, the guy who is Mr. Right now turns out to be "Mr. Wrong" later on. Your needs are going to change, and some of the kinds of things that make you happy and feel loved are going to change, too. Just think: Isn't it wonderful to realize that you will have lots of experiences of feeling "in love" before you settle down?

Why do females go against other females?
Roberta, age 14

During adolescence, girls usually want to spend more and more time with their peers forming friendships. Part of this process involves deciding who you want to be friends with and who you don't want to be friends with. During this time, your choices will often change dramatically and rapidly. As a result, at some point during your teen years, you will probably feel excluded or pushed out of a group or clique, or you will feel hurt, neglected, or disappointed by one of your friends. Even though this all happens to boys too, it is believed that because boys focus so much on activities, like sports or clubs, and measure their worth through their abilities, their competitiveness in friendships is not as great as it is for girls. While girls do care about their performance abilities, relationships are so important to them that exclusion and rejection among girls remains one of the most stressful parts of the teenage years.

Usually, as girls mature in their high school years, they have a keener perspective on how painful it can be to suffer betrayals and hurtful actions from friends. They have a stronger sense of who they are as individuals and don't rely as much on social standing alone to feel secure. They base their friendship choices less on "who is in, who is out, and how can I make sure that I am in?" and more on trust, loyalty, and shared interests. Probably, the same value that is responsible for some of the tension and conflict in young girls' friendships is responsible for some of the wonderful support older teens give each other— women tend to care intensely about their relationships!

* * *

One of the hardest times in a girl's life is the middle-school years, when cliques begin to form. This is a time when girls can be very mean to each other as they try desperately to "belong" to the right group. This meanness stems from an insecurity that many girls feel during their early teens. However, by the time they reach high school, girls increasingly become more open and friendly with each other. They find friends who share similar interests, like art, volunteering, drama, sports, languages, and so on, and are not as concerned about belonging to a specific group or clique. So, don't get too discouraged about female competition. Women are appreciating each other more and more. Even if it is not happening right now, it will change later on. You can start on that path and model this for your friends by supporting their strengths and abilities.

Why do other girls not like me when they don't even know me? *Janie, age 15*

Any girl who concludes that she doesn't like you without knowing you is a person who does not feel good about herself. When people don't like themselves, their jealousy and envy are reflected in their thoughts and behavior. As human beings, we have a tendency to compare ourselves with others, particularly others who are similar to ourselves. Typically, teens will compare themselves with other teens (even those they don't know) and use what they see as a guide for things such as how they should think, act, and even look. Some adolescent girls are very unhappy with parts of themselves. Many of them are strongly influenced by the ideal image that society presents for how females should look and behave. One way for a girl to try to feel better about herself is to devalue (or "put down") another female ("I think, act, or look better than you!"). While at the time these put downs may make her feel better, they are only a temporary solution for a deeper problem of low self-esteem.

So, don't take it personally when a girl dislikes you when she doesn't even know you. It is not due to any inadequacies within you! Those who judge you without knowing you really need help with a larger problem: their poor self-esteem. When you feel good about yourself, you perceive others in a positive light as well.

* * *

Lots of people make snap judgments based on very little information. In some ways, this can be a useful skill because it can assist them in making quick decisions when they need to. But it can also be a mistake! When someone decides that they don't like you, based on little or no information, they not only hurt your feelings but, if they do this a lot, they will eventually be seen as a snob. So, their behavior will wind up backfiring on them. There's probably very little you can do to change people who are like this, but you can protect yourself better by not chasing them and leaving yourself vulnerable to being rejected. Sometimes, we convince ourselves that the person who seems to ignore us most is the person we "have to" have as a friend. So you need to let go of the "have to" and pursue friends who don't make snap judgments about others.

Hot Tips

☞ Teen girls can be really mean, but you can't control other people. How *you* treat people will eventually get you lasting and trusting friendships.

☞ Have you been rejected by someone who doesn't even know you? She or he is probably very insecure and trying to feel "one up." Ignore her or him and move on. It's her or his loss.

☞ Get up your courage and ask that "special" guy out! The worst that can happen is that he says no—everyone gets rejected sometimes.

☞ A good boyfriend respects you, is fun to be with, and is someone you can really talk to. Don't settle on just any guy—you're worth too much!

☞ You're most likely to meet "Mr. Right" by getting involved in activities *you* enjoy. That's where you'll find guys you have something in common with.

☞ "Boy-crazy" girls don't have their own identity. They depend on having a guy to feel like a whole person.

☞ Boyfriends can come and go, but girlfriends often last forever. Take care of your friendships.

☞ Does your boyfriend insist that you choose between him and your girlfriends? Dump him! Don't let him control your life.

4

Guys, Love, and Sex—
How Do I Decide What to Do?

I have a serious boyfriend, and he wants to have sex. I'm not sure if I'm ready for it yet. What if he cheats on me? If he breaks up with me after we have sex, my life will be ruined. Mostly I feel like I really want to make him happy, but sometimes I wonder if I should go out with other guys. Maybe I'm too dependent on him? Sometimes I wonder what would happen If I broke up with him. What if he got really angry? What if I never meet anyone else? I think I want to stick with him, but I'm not sure I'm making the right decision. I'm so confused.—*Kim*

Why does it seem that all boys want is sex?
Brenda, age 14

Adolescence is a time when both girls and boys begin developing sexually and start becoming more attracted to and interested in the opposite sex. But sometimes it does seem as if boys are interested only in sex. While some may argue that there are biological differences between males and females that make males want or "need" sex more than females, this difference is more likely due to the ways that males and females are raised and how other people expect them to act. Even though many people believe men and women are equal, our society still has different expectations about what are appropriate attitudes and behaviors for males and females. On the topic of sex, males are expected to be more interested in sexual activity. Girls, on the other hand, are expected to be interested in interpersonal relationships and in fact are often socialized to believe that "good" girls don't want to have sex.

While these expectations don't influence all boys and girls, some boys do feel pressure to conform. They may really be interested in having meaningful interpersonal relationships but may feel that to be a "man," they have to want to and try to have sex, and thus they pretend that relationships are of little concern to them. Starting off by being friends with a boy can be very helpful in making sure that your needs for an interpersonal relationship are in balance with his needs for a physical relationship.

* * *

Boys in our culture feel a lot of pressure to be sexually active with girls—it is one of the ways boys prove to other boys that they are "men." Thus, in addition to the surge of sexual feelings because of hormones and body changes during adolescence, there are also social pressures for boys to perform sexually. At the same time, boys are taught to be less comfortable seeking emotional intimacy, so they use sex as a way to express their longings for closeness. But remember, boys vary tremendously in their ability to talk about their feelings and their sexual needs. That's why it's pretty important to know the particular boy you are interested in as a friend first. It is also really important for you to pay attention to your own needs and comfort zones. Girls and boys often have very different feelings around sexuality, and it is essential that you treat your own feelings with respect and expect that others will, too.

Not that I am going to do this soon, but I need some more help to understand sex.
Paula, age 12

Wow, isn't it funny that we hear so much about sex and see so many "sexy" things on TV and in the movies, but it is so hard to get any really good information about sex? Sometimes friends aren't very helpful, and it is kind of embarrassing to ask about specific stuff. Parents usually overreact to questions and think that you want to know so you can have sex. Even if you are lucky enough to have a good relationship with your mom or dad, they are often too embarrassed to talk openly about the subject. So, it can be very difficult to get help.

However, there are places where you can get some good and accurate information. Try talking with an older sibling, a school counselor, psychologist, school nurse, or teacher you trust. They can usually direct you to some good information. Another good place to start is with your doctor. Your doctor can be of help to you by answering your questions or telling you where you can find the information you want. You might be embarrassed, but doctors talk about this stuff all the time. So, even though it may feel awkward to you, you are better off in the long run getting the information you need rather than not knowing.

* * *

Of course you want to know about sex! Most kids your age have lots of questions and often have a hard time figuring out where they can get the answers. Other kids may act like they have all the answers, but they don't. There are many sources of accurate and good information, but many kids your age initially feel too embarrassed, so you might want to start by getting some information privately. The best place to do this is at your local library. When you go to the card catalogue or the computer, check out topics such as "sex," "female body," "male body," "reproduction," "physical development," or "health." Look for listings that don't sound too technical. Find a comfortable seat, and give yourself some time to begin your research. If there is a specific thing you want to look up, check the index at the back of the book or do a computer search to find the exact topic you are looking for.

If you have a computer at home and aren't concerned about your privacy, you don't even have to leave your house to do your Internet research. Once you feel a little more comfortable, you are more likely to be able to talk with others about your questions and concerns.

Why do I always feel like I should be pleasing the guy even though I don't get anything in return? *Adrienne, age 16*

Many girls have been raised to think that their job in a relationship with a guy is to make the guy happy. This is not right! Healthy relationships are a "give-and-take." Each person in the relationship should be concerned about the needs and wants of the other. There should be a balance so both people feel equal. If you feel that you are in a relationship where your needs and wants are not being met, reconsider why you are in this relationship. You deserve to be with someone who is as concerned about pleasing you as you are about pleasing him.

* * *

In our society, girls and women are taught from an early age to be nurturing, generous, giving, considerate of others' needs, sympathetic, and loving. However, they are *also* often taught to suppress their own needs and wants, deny their own emotions such as anger and sexual desire, and be completely "unselfish." When girls do this, they often wind up feeling like they have "lost themselves" in their efforts to please others. Your awareness of the pressure you feel to "be pleasing" is a crucial step in learning to voice your own needs, wants, and desires.

Many young women feel that if they assert themselves in relationships, they will be rejected. So, they give and give love in hopes of getting some in return. I often hear girls say, "If I just love him enough and give to him unconditionally, he'll change (meaning he'll give me what I need)." This rarely works, because when one person is sacrificing her or his *self* for the other person, that only leaves *one person* in the relationship. A healthy, satisfying relationship requires two people, both of whom have opinions, desires, needs, and wants that they are willing to share with the other. Self-sacrifice leads to happy endings only in the movies. In real-life relationships, it does not work.

If a teenager decides to have sex, what should she do about her parents? Should she tell them or what? *Natalia, age 15*

Under ideal circumstances, by the time you are a teenager, you will have already been talking with your parents about sex for many years. If this were true, initiating a conversation about sexual activity with them would be relatively easy and natural. But the reality is that most parents have a difficult time talking with their children about sexual behaviors and sexual decisions. It is often difficult for parents to accept that their teenager is thinking about having sex. Of course, whether you have had conversations with your parents in the past or not, you very likely have some sense of their values regarding sexual activity. If you anticipate that your parents are not going to support you becoming sexually active, it will be extremely difficult to talk about sex with them. If you feel that such a conversation is impossible, seek out another trustworthy adult to talk to.

It is also important to talk to your doctor so you can take the necessary steps to protect your health. Becoming sexually active involves some risks. You need to protect yourself from STDs (sexually transmitted diseases) and pregnancy. You need to evaluate your own motives and expectations *and* the possible emotional consequences of becoming sexually active. If you engage in sexual behavior that goes against *your own* beliefs and values, you are likely to feel very bad about yourself afterward. If you don't use proper protection, you could find yourself very anxious and worried for months until you find out if you are OK. Deciding to become sexually active should never be "an accident." It is an important decision that requires thought, planning, and honest communication with your partner.

* * *

Clearly, you are concerned about your parents' reactions. But much more important than the decision about telling them or not telling them is your own sense of clarity and peace with yourself about the decisions you are making. If you have carefully thought through your decision and paid attention to the consequences, including precautions to have safe sex, you are much more likely to be able to handle your parents. If you choose to tell them and feel good about your decision, whether they are accepting or rejecting, you will still be OK.

What happens when or if I have a boyfriend who wants to have sex, and I don't? How should I tell him? *Ruth, age 13*

One of the most important parts of a romantic relationship is communication. Telling the other person how you feel, what you want to do and what you do not want to do, whether it is a social activity or a sexual activity, is what makes a relationship work. Talk with your boyfriend and tell him straight out that you don't want to have sex. Then talk about what you *do* want to do together, which may or may not include kissing and touching. What is most important is that you really be aware of and stick with how *you* feel.

Sometimes girls are afraid to tell their boyfriends that they don't want to have sex, because they think their boyfriends might break up with them. Well, this may be a possibility. But having sex just to keep a relationship going does not take into account your feelings, and so you will be very unhappy.

* * *

The first thing you need to know is that you have a right to say "No" to anything that makes you feel uncomfortable. Don't ever let a guy convince you to engage in any physical activity that doesn't feel right to you. No matter what he says, or how he tries to persuade you, it is your obligation and responsibility *to yourself* to stick to what is right for you. The best way to tell him is to be honest, direct, and clear. It may seem blunt, or even rude, but you need to worry about *you*, not him.

You should also be aware that guys sometimes feel "teased" by girls. If a girl behaves as if she is going to have sex with a guy and then suddenly says "No," it is much more likely to mess up the relationship than if you are clear from the beginning. On the other hand, you might be confused about your feelings and start to act sexual, but then change your mind halfway through. If this happens, even though it might be very difficult and make the guy mad, you still have the right to say "No." Having sex with a guy is something you should be absolutely clear about before you do it.

Does the woman have the right to say no to a man? *Helen, age 12*

Yes! A woman has the right to say no to a man about anything she feels uncomfortable or unsure about. Saying no can be very difficult, especially if you are interested in maintaining the relationship. For some teen girls, saying no is extra difficult when they are involved in a relationship with a boy. Many girls have been brought up by families and in a culture that has made them feel that they should be submissive to men. In addition, some girls don't feel good enough about themselves or their feelings to realize that they have the right to say no. Relationships should be mutually respectful. If a boy wants or pressures you to think and behave differently than what you really feel, he is not respecting you. If you feel that you are in a relationship where you are not being respected, where your opinions or thoughts are not valued, you might want to reevaluate whether or not to continue in the relationship. Both girls and boys have the right to be in relationships where offering their true opinion and being respected when they say no does not put the relationship at risk.

* * *

Yes! You have the right to say no at any time, at any place, and at any point, even if you previously said yes. You can say no before, during, or the next time you are in that situation. And, you have the right to expect respect for your decision.

Sometimes there are situations that make it difficult for a young woman to say no, even when she really wants to. I have talked with young women who have, under the influence of drugs or alcohol, done things that they would have otherwise said no to. And, I have talked with women who said no and their no was not respected. There is also a more subtle but very powerful force that influences many teen girls. Because of the messages girls are given, many teen girls feel that men are entitled to sex and therefore they wind up engaging in sexual behaviors that really don't feel right. Guys are no more entitled to have their way than you are! So, if a guy wants to have sex with you, and this is not something you want, it is important for you to communicate exactly how you feel.

If he still insists and forces you to have sex, this is called rape! Be sure to remember that men who force girls to have sex against their will don't fit any particular profile. He may not "look evil." He may not wear black clothing and walk around in a trench coat. He may not be the "bad kid in school." In fact, he could be the most popular kid in the class, or the captain of the soccer team, or the nerdy musician. Or just about anyone! So, because you can't predict who a rapist could be from a guy's reputation or looks, it is even more important that you be as thoughtful as possible about the people you spend your time with and the places you go. This is one of the best ways to avoid getting into situations in which saying no might be ignored or violated.

It is always a good idea to know where a phone is and to carry enough money for a cab ride home. In fact, before you ever go out with a guy alone, be sure you've spent enough time getting to know what he is really like. And because you can't always know what is going to happen, remind yourself that no matter where you are, you have the right to leave. In the end, others will respect you more and, most importantly, you will like and respect yourself.

Why is it that when a guy has sex with a girl, he is called a "stud," but the girl is considered a "slut"? *Veronica, age 13*

Not everyone feels that way. But those who do are stuck in the past, in a time when men had all the rights. Some guys also feel that if they put girls down, it will be easier to push them around. If a guy can make a girl think of herself as a slut, it won't be so hard to push her around and tell her what to do. Some men make women feel so bad about themselves that they are afraid to leave an awful relationship. And that is a *big* mistake. Never stay in a relationship that makes you feel bad about yourself.

* * *

It is important to remember that these are labels that our society has made up. Our society gives permission to boys to express their sexual feelings. You could even say it "rewards" boys who have sexual experiences. The belief that having sex with girls proves to others that a boy is a real man is a powerful one, and also a problem, because it makes it hard for boys to be aware of how they are really feeling or to express their emotions. The other side of the coin is that girls are not supposed to have or express their sexual feelings. If she does, then she often is punished by being labeled a "slut."

Our society has given sex to boys and taken it from girls. But all of us have sexual feelings, because it is part of being human. This whole system has worked to keep girls from having power in relationships by making sure they continue to be treated as sex objects. These ideas have contributed to keeping girls down. You can help to change the way our society treats girls by reminding yourself that decisions about your sexual behavior are *yours* and by actively deciding what is right for you.

How can girls prevent sexual abuse? How do you know if you are getting into an abusive situation? *Lucy, age 14*

Girls cannot always prevent sexual abuse. Sometimes there are situations in which the guy is much more powerful than the girl, and the girl is afraid and feels that she cannot say no. At other times, the guy is older and tries to manipulate the girl by leading her to believe things that are not true. For example, an older guy might tell you that you are "supposed to have sex with an older guy so you can learn from someone with more experience." Sometimes, a teen girl can be struggling so hard with issues of her own self-worth, such as her attractiveness or whether or not she is worth loving, that even though she knows she is being abused, she cannot seem to stay away from the abuser. In all of these examples, it is not her fault if she is sexually abused. It is the guy's responsibility not to abuse girls. If you are in an abusive relationship, don't wait! Get help from an adult you trust.

Here are some danger signs:

- A boy who is very controlling and insists that you always do what he says.
- A boy who is extremely jealous and "goes off of the deep end" if you ever look at another guy. Often the jealousy goes so far that he accuses you of being with someone else when you haven't been.
- A boy who is possessive of you and gets angry when you spend time with other friends or with your family. He wants you to spend time with him exclusively. He doesn't even want to do things with other couples when he is with you.
- A boy who won't take no for an answer. He doesn't get that "No" is a complete sentence and just keeps pushing.
- A boy who is very charming and nice only when he wants something. He uses being nice as a strategy to get you to do something he wants.

- A boy who is verbally or physically abusive. Beware of guys who belittle you and make you feel worthless, especially guys who hit you! Many of these guys also put the blame for the abuse on you, saying that you brought it on because you didn't do something right.

* * *

There are usually warning signs that indicate that someone is or could be abusive. And knowing the warning signs could actually save your life!

- Are you in a relationship with someone who is extremely jealous and wants to control where you go, who you see, and what you do?
- Does he expect you to be the perfect girlfriend and devote all of your time to him?
- Does he try to keep you from other activities that do not revolve around him?
- Does he blame you or others for his feelings and behaviors rather than taking responsibility for his own actions?
- Does he "rant and rave" about relatively minor incidents like getting a traffic ticket or getting a poor grade on a school assignment?
- Is he cruel to animals or children?
- Does he seem indifferent to the pain and suffering of others?
- Does he call you or others degrading names or say other cruel and hurtful things?

- Does he break things or strike objects when he is angry?
- Has he ever slapped or hit you or someone else?
- Has he ever physically restrained you?

If you answered yes to any of these questions, you could be at risk! Talk to someone who can help you evaluate the amount of risk that you are in. Call a local support line for resources in your town. Talk to an adult you trust. Don't wait!

* * *

Even if you are not in a relationship, abuse can occur on a first date or with someone you just met. Pay attention to how you can avoid getting into dangerous situations. You can do this by being cautious about your physical surroundings. Do you know where you are so that you can get out of the room or situation quickly and find a safe place? Are there other people around who would hear you if you called for help?

One of the most common things that an abuser uses to control women is alcohol or drugs; "getting you drunk or high" may sound like a cliché, but it happens, and it happens a lot. The person offering you drinks or drugs may be doing so just to control you more easily. Alcohol and drugs impair you physically and mentally. The abuser knows this and is usually watching and waiting for you to lose control. Especially on a first date, but even with someone you know, drinking or using drugs can put you at a very high risk.

Unfortunately, even if you do everything you can to prevent sexual abuse, it is still possible that something terrible could happen. If something happens to you, it is important to get medical help *immediately*. Tell someone *right away* so that the abuse can be stopped and you can get the help you need. Most importantly, remember that you cannot control everything in the world and it is *not your fault*. Even if you look back and think that you could have used better judgment, the other person is still responsible for his behavior, and it is never acceptable for him to abuse you sexually, physically, or emotionally.

I took my boyfriend back after he cheated on me because I think we can work it out. Does this mean that I have low self-esteem? *Colleen, age 17*

If you are accepting him back only because you *want to believe* that he won't cheat again, then perhaps your decision is based more on insecurity and fear of loss and loneliness than on anything he has done to convince you that you can trust him again. If this is the case, and you take him back, your self-esteem will suffer, especially if he goes on to disrespect you and not treat you well. Aren't you deserving of a partner who will be loyal, caring, and true to you? Maybe this is why you are wondering whether your decision is a reflection of low self-esteem.

However, there are also many couples who experience an episode of cheating and do work it out successfully. In fact, for some couples, being willing and able to work through a serious problem like this is a sign of strength, not failure. So, the important thing is not just whether or not you accept him back after he cheats, but how you come to your decision. This is why you want to focus on how he handles the situation, his pattern of trustworthiness, and his reasons for cheating in the first place. Accepting him back may be reasonable if

1. He has sincerely apologized.
2. He has taken the situation seriously and convinced you that he has every intention of never doing it again.
3. He has a history of being dependable and respectful.

Because respect, trust, and communication are so important in relationships, absolutely insisting on these qualities is one of the best ways you can build and ensure your self-esteem.

* * *

Your *willingness* to work things out with your boyfriend is not an indicator of low self-esteem. Your *reasons* for wanting to work it out, however, may have some association with how you feel about yourself. It hurts a lot to find out that your boyfriend has cheated. It is normal to feel depressed and angry. It is also common to have self-doubts such as, "Was I not good enough?" or "Did I do something to cause this?" It may take time to heal from this wound, whether or not you and your boyfriend stay together. During that time, it is important that you evaluate the relationship.

- What are you getting out of it?
- Is this relationship meeting your needs for companionship, support, and love?
- Is your boyfriend willing to work on rebuilding the trust that has been broken?
- Do the two of you agree on the degree of commitment and faithfulness that you want and expect from each other?

The ability to forgive someone is a strength, not a weakness. Forgiveness, however, does not require being a "doormat." Forgiveness should be based on an honest evaluation of the other person's sincere desire and commitment to changing her or his behavior and not betraying you again.

How can you avoid letting a painful break-up consume you and destroy your whole life? *Lizzie, age 17*

There is no avoiding it; there will be pain. Lots of it. When you love someone and lose them, it's painful. It's like any loss, which means it takes time, lots of time, to get over it. Even if it takes a year or so, it doesn't mean that it won't get better. But there are some things that can definitely help:

- Talk about it with friends and with an adult you trust who can really listen.
- Go out with your friends and your family, even if you don't feel like it.
- Find ways to distract yourself, if only for a short time, like a video or music that's not related to the relationship.
- Go for walks; exercise helps.
- Keep a journal about how you're feeling.
- Say nice things to yourself, particularly those things you believed about yourself while you were in the relationship—they are still true even though you don't feel them now.

If you don't find yourself feeling better and you've lost interest in everything and are having trouble concentrating and feel really down, find a mental health professional, such as a psychologist, you can talk to. Find a therapist who knows how other 17-year-olds have felt after a painful break-up.

* * *

There's no doubt about it—if this was an important relationship, there is no way to avoid feeling traumatized by the break-up. Someone who has been a very important part of your life is gone, and there is a big hole from the loss. This is the exact time when you should turn to your friends and family for support and comfort. You may feel lots of different emotions, including anger, numbness, and hurt. And these feelings might come out in many different ways, like being irritable with a sibling, not being able to concentrate or focus on schoolwork, sleeping all the time, or not being able to sleep at all. You'll probably shed a lot of tears, but the tears are part of the healing process. All of these feelings and reactions are normal and will diminish as time passes. Use your support systems to help you through the trauma. Distract yourself with other activities. Keep busy, exercise, and remind yourself that even though it feels like you'll never meet anyone else, you will. Just give it some time.

Should adolescent girls have long-term relationships, or is it healthier to see more guys in this period of time? *Rena, age 16*

You've asked a great and a tough question. And the answer depends on your definitions of "long-term" and "healthier." On the one hand, there is nothing wrong or "unhealthy" about having the same boyfriend for a while. In fact, unless you have enough time with the same boyfriend, you may not have the chance to really get to know him and to learn what you do and don't want in a boyfriend.

On the other hand, if you have the same boyfriend for too long, like all through high school, you'll miss out on the opportunity to date different guys and compare how you feel in different relationships. Many adults who have had only one or two relationships before they got married say they regret that they didn't use their teen and young adult years to learn more about themselves in relationships with different people. Your teen years are a time for exploring many things, including relationships with guys.

So, while long-term relationships are not necessarily unhealthy, if a single relationship lasts so long that you wind up having limited experiences with other guys, you might want to think about what you might be missing. You will have many, many years to be in a long-term committed relationship, so why "settle down" when you're so young?

* * *

Once in a while, a girl meets someone when she is young, falls in love, and "lives happily ever after." But more often, teenage girls are not ready for long-term relationships. They need more time to learn about what they really want in life and what they really are looking for in a relationship. What is important is to have the freedom to explore who you are, what you want your life to be like, and to be able to experiment with different identities. If you find a relationship with one guy that still gives you the freedom to explore yourself and learn and grow, the relationship could last a lifetime. But, if the relationship doesn't allow you that amount of freedom, you'll need to move on.

Hot Tips

☞ There are no ifs, ands, or buts about it. You *always* have the right to say no to a guy!

☞ Girls are just as interested in sex as guys are. But guys are *allowed* to show it, while girls aren't. It's normal and healthy to be interested in sex.

☞ Your boyfriend has cheated on you? If you're not totally convinced he's *really* sorry, don't take him back. He'll probably do it again!

☞ There's no way around it, breaking up hurts a lot! Talk to friends and family and keep busy. Time is a great healer.

☞ Want to know more about sex? Check out the library and Web sites. Talk to your doctor, older siblings, or other trusted adults—even your parents.

☞ Stay *far away* from guys who are controlling, jealous, possessive, or verbally or physically abusive —*they are dangerous!*

☞ If you've been physically or sexually abused, tell someone *now!* No matter how it happened, *it's not your fault!*

☞ Expect your boyfriend to treat you with the same care and consideration you give him. Demand equal treatment—you deserve it.

☞ You can't know what you really want in a guy unless you've had lots of experience. A steady boyfriend is fine for a while, but don't miss out on learning from a variety of relationships.

5

School, School, School—Why Is There Always a Problem?

I'm having such a hard time with my school-work. I want to get good grades, but I'm just not one of the really smart kids. Sometimes it's really hard to concentrate, and I get so stressed out. It isn't fair that I have to work so hard to do well. Lots of other kids don't take school seriously; they don't even try. Sometimes I just want to give up, but I know that won't get me anywhere. — *Samantha*

Why do girls take their work much more seriously and why are they more sensitive about their grades? *Sonya, age 12*

While it isn't always true that girls take their work more seriously than boys, in middle school and high school it is generally true. First of all, girls tend to be about a year and a half to two years more developmentally advanced than boys. This means that girls have usually thought more about their future after high school than boys. They realize that performance in high school is related to their future goals, like getting into college or getting a good job. Boys, on the other hand, don't usually think past high school. They are much more likely to be living only for the present.

A second reason why teenage girls seem to care more about grades is that they are more into pleasing their parents and teachers. Research shows that, during their teen years, girls tend to have better relationships with their parents than boys. Boys are expected to become independent sooner than girls. Often boys feel they must begin to push away from their parents and the system long before a girl might. A boy doesn't want to be considered a "wuss."

A third reason is that school is considered a "feminine institution." This means that more feminine types of behaviors are required for success, and most of the teachers are women. For example, boys need to move around more than girls. So, sitting still and paying attention for many hours can be much harder for them. Boys tend to have more difficulty than girls succeeding in such a system, and they "turn off" more.

Finally, girls appear to be more sensitive (they are not) than boys because they are more willing to show their feelings in front of others. Therefore, when a girl gets a bad grade, she may get very upset and cry, whereas a boy may feel as bad, but he is less likely to show it in public. Don't assume that boys don't care just because they don't show it.

Why is school so hard? *Thelma, age 13*

For many teens, it seems that all at once the content and requirements of courses in school become complicated and overwhelming. At the same time, much more responsibility for learning is put on the student. All this is a way of preparing you for life. During the teen years, your brain is maturing in ways that allow you to handle more abstract and complex academic material. Schoolwork that you could do without much effort in the past, because you easily understood it the first time in class, may now require a lot more time. You may have to listen harder, read more, study more, and have a chance to discuss the material before you're able to really "get" it. This can be both frustrating and overwhelming. But it is also very gratifying when you finally do get it.

* * *

Believe it or not, school is really not designed to be difficult! And the educational curriculum was not purposely set up to make school hard for you. Throughout the years, educators have been working hard to determine the best grade level to introduce different learning materials to kids. However, this does not always work well for everyone for several reasons:

- Not all students are ready to learn the same things at the same age, because kids learn at different rates.
- If students didn't totally understand something in one grade or subject, like how to do fractions, they can run into trouble later on when knowing how to do fractions is necessary for being able to do a higher level of math.
- Some students have trouble concentrating in school because of problems at home or with their friends.
- Some students find middle school and high school much harder because their teachers encourage and expect them to think for themselves more and more each year.

Making the transition from being dependent on parents and other adults as thinkers for you to thinking for yourself is not always an easy task, but it is a necessary one to help you become a successful and independent adult.

What can I do to help myself with all my stress with school? *Jessica, age 18*

You're not alone. According to recent studies, many teens today find school very stressful. Parents and teachers put a great deal of emphasis on the importance of grades for your future success. And, besides schoolwork, there are so many other things you're probably involved with, like sports or other school activities, community service, helping out at home, and maybe even a part-time job. So, it's no surprise that teens today feel so much more stressed than they did a generation ago.

Let's look at some of the ways you can reduce your stress about school. The first thing you need to do is to ask yourself some very important questions. So take a few minutes to think about these:

- Am I trying to do more than I can possibly do?
- Am I a perfectionist—do I have trouble accepting the fact that I can't be good at everything? Am I able to feel good simply about doing my very best?
- Do I feel afraid or embarrassed to ask for help when I need it?
- Am I so focused on or worried that I either don't take time out to unwind or relax, or do I do the opposite—do I procrastinate and avoid schoolwork and then try to pull things off at the last minute?

If you answered "yes" to one or more of these questions, then it's time to make some changes if you want to reduce your stress. Here are some ideas that might help:

- Look carefully at all the demands on your time, and make a list of the most important to the least important. Then decide on one thing that, even though you might really like to do it, you will consider not doing right now because you really can't fit it into your life if you want to be less stressed.

- Learn about time management. Most teens (and many adults) could get a lot more done and have more free time if they learned some basic time management skills. Check your school or local library for some books or tapes about time management. Here is one time management tip to get you going. Each night, make a list of what you need to do for the next day and write down how long you think each one will take. Then, make up a schedule for the next day. At the end of the day, look at how well you stuck to your schedule and see if your time estimates were right.

- Try to first do the things you dislike most. Getting the worst stuff out of the way first will help you feel less stressed.

- Take short breaks when you're working and move around. A brisk walk or run will definitely help you feel less stressed.

- Most of all, remind yourself that doing your best is all you can do, and reward yourself for your efforts!

* * *

It is very important to learn to cope with stress, because stress can negatively affect your performance. There are several different stress management techniques that can be useful. Relaxation is an important one: You can learn to relax your body physically while still focusing your mind. Some people do muscle relaxation exercises; others find meditation or yoga exercises helpful.

Here's a technique called *visualization*. Take a few moments to close your eyes and picture a calm, happy scene. Let yourself imagine all the details of this scene—the sights, sounds, smells, and textures. Focus on your relaxed feelings. When you open your eyes again, try to keep feeling relaxed.

If relaxation exercises don't help, you might need to think about decreasing the level of stress by changing your circumstances. Speak to your teacher if you need help with a particular subject; speak to your guidance counselor to find out whether you should change your course load. The worst thing to do is to just let the stress mount up until it feels overwhelming and you burn out.

Why can't I concentrate on schoolwork sometimes? *Christine, age 16*

For some adolescents, it looks like anything is more important than schoolwork! Imagine a girl sitting in math class right before lunch. The teacher is droning on and, although she is trying to listen, it seems impossible because of all of the other thoughts in her head, like

Only five more minutes until lunch; will Trevor walk by? What should I be doing when he comes down the

91

hall? Should I talk to him after what he said yesterday? Do I look OK? I gotta run and comb my hair. Will he notice the new zit on my face? I feel really bad about this math class. I just don't get it. I'm really worried about getting a "C." It will really mess up my average. The teacher is a dweeb, so boring. I know my mom is still angry about the jacket I loaned to Jessica. Jessica lost it, not me, but I shouldn't have yelled back at my mom like that. I shouldn't have told Carrie about Melissa and Jim because I think she told Melissa. Melissa is being a brat to me. What should I do about Melissa; she is a good friend, and I don't want to lose her. What about this weekend, will my friends hang out with Trevor and his friends? I really worry about all the drinking. I don't want to drink that much, but I don't want Trevor to think that I can't handle it.

Is this the kind of stuff that goes on inside your head, too? It is for many teens, and it sure makes concentrating on schoolwork difficult.

The good news is that you *can* improve your power of concentration by working on it. You can control the thoughts that come into your mind and get in the way of paying attention. Try this: As soon as you become aware that you are not concentrating, take three deep breaths. Inhale slowly through your nose and take in as much air as you can. Then hold your breath for about three seconds. Now exhale through your mouth slowly, as if you were blowing on a teaspoon full of hot tea. When you exhale, imagine that you are blowing out all of your distracting thoughts.

Another technique is to wear a rubber band around your wrist. Now, snap it! Say to yourself, "I have a choice from now on. I am going to throw out all of the thoughts racing through my mind and focus on the class work." Every time you find your mind wandering, do the same thing. When you snap the rubber band on your wrist, imagine that you are slamming all the doors to your mind shut so the random thoughts can't get back in. Don't give any of those random thoughts any airtime. As soon as you find yourself thinking them, repeat the exercise. Then, if you have successfully been able to bring yourself back to concentrating, reward yourself when you get home. Because you concentrated in class, you can have half an hour on the phone with your friend. The trick is not to allow yourself a reward unless you really earn it!

How come I feel discouraged when I am in a classroom full of people who are way smarter than me? Azina, age 17

It sounds as if you are comparing your abilities with everyone else in the class. Let's deal with the issue of comparing first. It is very normal to compare ourselves with others—it is one of the ways we figure out how we are doing at something. For example, let's say you took an American History test and received a score of 62 out of 100. How do you know whether or not that is a good score or a bad score unless you find out what the class average was? Let's say the class average was 45; now you know that you did very well on this test! The trick in comparing is to make sure that you are comparing yourself with the right people and that you are using the right measures for what you are comparing.

Back to our example. Suppose you find out that the class average of 45 on the American History test was from a class of college students. Because college students are supposedly more advanced than high school students, your score of 62 now looks even better. There's another factor that you have to consider in this comparison process. Suppose you discover that 35 of the test questions are not about American History but are about Eastern Europe in the 17th century. If this is true, the test is not a fair measure of what you know about American History. What all this means is that you must be sure that you are comparing yourself fairly.

Now, what do you tell yourself *after* you have compared yourself with others? What if you really do fall at or near the bottom? If you are feeling terrible about your position in the class, you might be saying to yourself, "Wow, dumbo, your test scores are worse than everyone else's in the class. You really must be stupid." Telling yourself things like this is never helpful and they are not true. Instead, try saying something like, "Learning the material in this class is *not* one of my strengths, but I'll do the best I can. Let me think of all the other areas that I have strengths in. Right now, when I'm feeling so bad, I need to look at the things I'm good at, and later on I can make a plan to improve my weaknesses." When any of us compare ourselves with others, if we are honest we will find that we are better in some areas and worse in others. The idea is to keep a positive attitude and remind yourself of your strengths.

Why is it that automatically some people are a lot smarter than others? *Monica, age 12*

As you already know, no two people are the same, and when it comes to being able to do schoolwork, some kids do have an easier time learning some subjects than learning others. And then there are those kids that seem to have an easy time learning everything. It can be really frustrating to feel like you have to work so much harder than other kids. While some kids do have it easy, the majority have to work pretty hard and consistently to do well in school. Most of the time, the difference between the kids who seem a lot smarter and the kids who have a hard time is that the "smarter kids" have an "I can" rather than an "I can't" attitude. We all have different skills and talents. Each of us needs to figure out our own gifts, interests, and passions and then be willing to work to develop them. No matter what it is, the more time and effort you put into things, the smarter you will feel.

Why is math and science harder for girls than boys? *Laura, age 14*

Math and science are *not* harder for girls than boys. The problem is that teen girls often have less confidence in their intellectual ability in general, and in math and science in particular, than boys. Studies that have examined the ability of males and females to complete math problems correctly show that both sexes perform about the same level except at the most advanced levels of math. In fact, during the elementary school years, girls are better at math computations than boys. However, beginning in high school and certainly in college, boys do surpass girls in the more advanced math classes. This happens because girls stop enrolling in higher level math classes in high school, and so by the time they reach college they are not as well prepared in math and science as boys are. Therefore, at the higher levels, girls do worse than boys in math and science courses.

Now, when girls do take the same number of math courses as boys, their achievement scores are similar. Although it looks like math and science are harder for girls than boys, it really has more to do with the classes they take than anything else. The problem is that usually, sometime during middle school, girls begin getting the message (sometimes indirectly) that they are not good at math. Instead, they are pushed to take classes that will prepare them for the more traditional occupations for women in our society, like teaching, nursing, and taking care of family. The majority of people still do not imagine women entering jobs in which they need a good math and science background. Don't fall into the trap. Push yourself and try some higher level math and science courses. Avoiding higher level math and science courses could limit your future job options and exclude you from many of the higher paying jobs. Remember that difficulty is all in your head. Girls can succeed at math and science courses just as easily as boys can!

What can I do to make myself more confident in sports? *Carmela, age 17*

Whether it is sports or something else, feeling more confident in your ability to do anything requires that you

- Make an honest assessment of your skill or knowledge about whatever it is that you want to feel more confident about.
- Set up an "action plan" to improve your skill or knowledge.
- Develop the patience and self-discipline to work slowly and steadily toward your goal.

Because your question is specifically about sports, let's look at some specific techniques that might be helpful to you.

- Eating right, getting enough sleep, and treating

your body with care are essential if you want to be able to do your best in any sport.

- Use "positive self-talk." This means that you work on "talking to yourself" with words and phrases that will help you stay motivated and focused on your goal. For example, let's say that soccer is your sport, and during the last game you missed a pass that you have been "kicking" yourself about for the past few days. Don't keep beating yourself up; learn to let go of the "miss." Concentrate instead on "I can" statements and phrases such as "I'm gonna score!"

- Remember that to increase your confidence in any sport you have to practice and practice and practice! And, while reading about a sport and watching others play can help, increasing your confidence will only come from getting out there. All good athletes "mess up" sometimes, but it's the ones who don't drown in their mistakes, who learn what they can from them and then pick themselves up and move on, who excel.

* * *

Excelling in sports can come from inborn talent, skill, or coordination. But a very big part comes from things that are much more in your control: the effort you put into it, the amount you practice, and your "image" of yourself as competent in sports. On the physical level, you can devote your spare time and energy to improving your skills. Speak to a coach about what particular drills you can practice that will help you improve. On the mental level, visualize your success in the sport, which can help change your self-image. You can learn techniques to help you concentrate and focus. Even watching others play can be helpful. There are lots of books available on how to develop the mental focus and confidence that might be useful. Check out the sports section in your library or local bookstore. You can also get lots of information on the Internet.

What would a healthy adolescent girl's study habits be like? *Jamie Ann, age 15*

I'm not exactly sure what you mean by "healthy," but let's consider what some girls have said that works for them, and you can see if any of these tips work for you.

- Find a place to study that is yours. It can be the dining room table, a desk somewhere, or your bed, but it's a place where you can focus and where you will always study.
- Approach your schoolwork with the idea that you will study every school night, and plan it in your schedule. Just because you don't have specific homework doesn't mean you don't need to review, study, or do work in advance. Each Sunday, prepare for the coming week by deciding which two hours you'll give each day for homework and studying.
- Pay attention to how your mind works. Do you do best just sitting down and doing the two hours

straight, or do you need breaks? If you need breaks, what kind of breaks get you back to studying feeling refreshed and what kind of breaks might upset you or get you off track? Learn which subjects are better for you to study alone and which ones are best learned with the help of friends or even parents.

- Learn which subject is best for you to start with. If you love English, should you leave it for last as your "treat," or start with it to get you revved up?
- Talk to your teachers to make sure you understand the assignments. Yes, even talk to the geeky teacher or the mean one who's always yelling.

It's all about your motivation, attitude, and effort. Studying is something you have to decide you want to do because it will get you where you want to go. It's an investment for your future.

How come some people think its cool to just sit around and not try their hardest in school? *Rita, age 14*

First you have to remember that when you see someone or something, you are only seeing the outside of the story—what is visible to you. It may look to you like some kids are content not to try, but that is probably not true. They may have had a lot of feedback and experiences that have made them feel that they are "no good" and "not smart" at schoolwork, and now they believe they are not smart enough to succeed in school. If someone kept telling you that you were not good enough, would you keep trying? Probably not, because it is common for people to believe what they are told, especially when they are young.

These kids want to be just as successful as anyone else, but they lack the "tools" to make this happen. These tools include parents who love them and care about them doing well in school and feedback that tells them that they are smart and can handle the work. They also need a positive sense of self-esteem that says that doing well in school is worth working for. When people "act cool" about failing, they are doing just that, acting. At the time, they may even believe that they do not care—and may have convinced themselves that being smart is not for them. Imagine what your life would be like if you had already convinced yourself that you were a failure. That would be a pretty sad way to live. These kids feel this way every day about their lives. You can help to ensure your own success by making connections with adults and friends who support your doing well in school, who give you positive feedback about your success and who also help you when you get stuck.

As an honors student always taking the most challenging classes with the same group of 30 others, have I missed any experiences social or otherwise? Have I been hurt at all by it? *Frieda, age 16*

There are many paths to take and choices to make, and each has its advantages and disadvantages. If there is any disadvantage to the honors program you described, it would lie more in the lack of diversity in your classroom than in the honors program itself. That is, you may be exposed to a smaller range of kids and therefore have less in the way of diverse social experiences and challenges. When you are exposed for a long time to a small group of peers, especially kids who are just like you, it limits the diversity of your experiences. To expand your experiences, make a special effort to join in on other activities, either in or outside of school, that include a broader range of kids than just those in your honors group. These might include a sport, a volunteer group, or a church youth group. Whenever you can, balance your choices by paying attention to the ways in which diversity can enrich your life. The very fact that you are aware and want to have more diverse relationships is wonderful, but it is certainly not necessary to sacrifice your honors program.

* * *

The reality is, yes, you probably have missed out on some other experiences. Every time you make a choice, you are choosing *not* to do something else. The important thing is to try to make smart choices. Smart choices are sometimes different from what other people think is best for you. Smart choices are not based on peer pressure, family expectations, or the easiest way out. Smart choices are those that fit who you are and your goals in life. So even though you might be missing out on other experiences, smart choices are making the best decisions you can—the ones that are right for you.

Hot Tips

☞ Everyone is born with different abilities, but in the long run, it's how much effort you put in that will determine your success.

☞ School is supposed to get harder and require more time as you get older. If you're really struggling, ask for help from your teachers or your parents. You're entitled to the help you need.

☞ While the kids who are blowing off school are probably having more fun at the moment, they will pay the price later on. Don't blow your chances for the future.

☞ You can learn good study habits by paying attention to how you learn. Try getting the hardest stuff over with first, and take some breaks as a reward.

☞ School is important, but so is having a life! All work and no play is no fun, and it's not healthy.

Try for balance—you'll be happier, and you won't burn out.

☞ You can improve your concentration skills with practice, but you'll have to work at it. Try out different ways and times for studying to see which one works best for you.

☞ While it's natural to compare yourself with others, it can also be very dangerous for your self-esteem. Use your grades as a way of seeing what *you* need to work on, not as a measure of your self-worth.

☞ It's a total myth that guys are better than girls in math and science. The reality is that girls get this message from other girls, guys, and even parents and teachers. Don't buy into it!

6

How Do I Find the Time to Do It All?

I have to pay for a lot of stuff myself, so I work after school to earn money. With my job, homework, and friends, I can't get my life organized and get everything done. My dad made up a schedule for me, but I can't seem to stick to it. There's just not enough time to do everything I need to do. Last week I fell asleep in my first period class, and my teacher got really pissed off. I don't know how to balance school, work, and my social life, but I can't give up any of it.
— *Jeanine*

Why is my life so disorganized? *Julia, age 15*

Between school, home, family, friends, and all the other things that you are committed to in your life, you're often being pulled in many directions at one time. With so many pulls on you and so little time, it is easy to get caught running from one thing in your life to another. Some things in your life have a rigid structure, like the time you spend in school, where there are strict time requirements. Other times, like when you are hanging out with your friends, there is probably very little structure. How to manage time and how to "structure" or organize yourself in a way that works for you are skills that are learned. They don't just come naturally. When you were younger, adults had much greater control of your time and how you did things. Now that you are older, you've got to start doing it yourself.

Getting organized doesn't need to take a lot of time or effort. First, observe your life and see what structures or routines might help. For instance, does the "getting ready for school" routine go much smoother for you if you pick out what to wear the night before? Where in your life are you "using up" a lot of your time? Are you watching too much TV or getting "lost" on the Internet? Would it help you to "power through" a bunch of tasks, like chores or homework, to get them over with, as opposed to avoiding them or dragging them out over time? Reflecting on these things in your life, setting up routines, and taking control of how you use your time can make a huge difference between feeling disorganized and out of control and feeling like you're steering your own ship.

* * *

Sometimes, life seems disorganized because there is simply too much to do, too many things to keep on top of. Someone once described her life as "organized chaos." This means that although you may wish that different parts of your life were more "in order," you have a lot going on and are managing quite well, as long as you don't get too picky. Think of a juggler who is juggling five or six balls at a time. If he stops to look down to see if his shoe laces are tied, he is sure to drop one or more of the balls. So, continue to focus on the important stuff, ignore the irrelevant stuff, and know that there will be a break sooner or later, and then you will have some time to tie up the loose ends.

Why do I feel as if there's not enough time during the day? *Tara, age 17*

In the last few years, your life has most likely become increasingly full as you've added on activities, responsibilities, and interests. All of these take up your time and energy, and it is easy to feel overwhelmed. For a couple of days, try keeping track of how you're spending each half-hour of your day. Make an objective assessment of how productively you used the time. For instance, if you "studied between 7 and 8 p.m.," assess whether that was productive, concentrated study time or whether you were doing other things (taking phone calls, daydreaming). If the latter is the case, you may be better off allotting several

15-minute periods for concentrated studying. The same would hold true for free time. Are you really enjoying your free time, or are you just filling it up with stuff that is really not that enjoyable to you? Observing yourself and objectively looking at your use of time will allow you to be more aware of how you might be using time inefficiently and to make changes that will allow you to accomplish more in a shorter period of time. It is also helpful to spend a few minutes thinking about your schedule at the start of each day. Then you will know what needs to be done and when you might have free time. At the end of the day, check in with yourself and review what worked and what didn't.

* * *

Not only do adults expect more and more from teenagers as they get older, but teenagers themselves have greater interests and become involved in more activities. You are becoming more independent and taking on more of your own pursuits, like part-time jobs, clubs, and social activities. At the same time, you are being given increased responsibilities at home and school. This can certainly feel overwhelming and make it difficult for you to prioritize all the demands on you. Things that used to be your top priorities, like homework or helping around the house, may not seem nearly as important as pursuing new experiences, like a steady boyfriend, an important position at school, or a part-time job. Trying to do everything that family and other adults expect of you while at the same time building and maintaining all your new relationships and interests is likely to feel draining. If you have done all you can to prioritize things and manage your time, and you still feel stressed, it probably means that something's got to go. Too much stress will take away from even the best things in your life.

How can you balance your life between social and scholarly activities? *Tracy, age 17*

Finding and maintaining a balance between work and play is like walking on a tightrope. You first have to get your balance and then concentrate on not losing it. For most teens the challenge is to balance friendships, family, school, and sports or hobbies. But this balancing act can be harder for girls than for boys, because girls often invest more time and energy in their friendships than boys do. Therefore, girls often feel more conflicted about what is most important to them, so prioritizing activities can be difficult. Because family, friends, and school continue to be important to most girls throughout adolescence, each of these areas needs time and attention. At times, academics may take primary importance (like just before exams or during the process of looking at colleges) while at other times, friends and social activities may receive more attention (like dating someone new, planning a trip with friends, or preparing for the prom). To find a balance among competing demands, it is important to recognize that all these things are very important, but it is impossible to attend to everything at the same time.

* * *

Close your eyes and imagine that you are on the beach at the ocean with your surfboard. The waves are coming at you. Each of these waves is one you want to ride, but you can't ride them all. You have to pick and choose. Finding a balance in life and deciding which "waves to ride" is not only something you have to deal with now but will always be part of your life. Balance is not only picking and choosing the wave to ride but also how long you ride it. In life, not everything should get equal time either. For example, one week might be filled with social activities, while academics are on the back burner. The next two weeks, you may find yourself having to say no to a bunch of social events cause it's time to focus on school. Don't let the waves catch you off guard and knock you down. *You* need to be in control and pick and choose the waves you ride and how long you stay on each of them.

How do you convince yourself to stick to a particular schedule? *Ann Marie, age 16*

Learning to plan and motivating yourself to staying with your plan is the job of a lifetime. It's ongoing. But let's start with a very important question.

Who made your schedule? If someone else made it for you, you are less likely to follow it. So the first step is to make your own schedule. You'll want to check some things out with other people, like your parents, who may need you to do things at specific times, or your friends, who may only be available at certain times. But the final schedule must be yours or it won't work. Next, you have to give yourself rewards for doing things on schedule. This means knowing what are "rewards" for you. If something on the schedule is really important, like studying for a history test, and you hate the subject, give yourself a big reward after you're done, like calling your best friend. In the beginning, you will probably underestimate or overestimate how long it will take you to do some things. But, with experience, your estimates will get better and better. Forgive yourself when you don't stay on schedule. Most kids and adults try to do way too much in a single day. Learning to stay on schedule is really hard—especially today, when everyone expects so much from you, like getting good grades, having friends, spending time with your family, exercising, and on and on. You simply can't do it all.

* * *

Try not to overwhelm yourself by trying to tackle too much at once. If you are having trouble finding the motivation to stick to your schedule, maybe you need to revise the schedule. Making your schedule more doable will help your motivation. How about taking one day at a time? So, if you make up a schedule for the next day, your goal is to do what you planned for that day. Sometimes we set ourselves up for failure by making promises, even to ourselves, that we can't keep. It is far better to make a small commitment and take it one day at a time. If you have a problem sticking to a schedule one day at a time, try an hour at a time. Whatever you set as your goal, pat yourself on the back when you complete it. Once you get comfortable with smaller goals, then you can make them bigger and build up to a schedule that is realistic, and one that you *want* to stick to.

What are the most efficient strategies for solving problems and making decisions?
Patty, age 16

The first step is to define what the problem is. This may sound silly, but often we try to "fix" something before we really have a clear handle on exactly what it is we are trying to fix. A good technique to get the problem clearer in your mind is to try writing it down in words. This will help you to clarify exactly what you are trying to solve or resolve. Once you've done this, decide what change or outcome you want. This will allow you to be "proactive" (take the lead) instead of simply reacting. It will also help give you direction and help you to stay focused on the outcome that you're hoping to accomplish. Once you know exactly where you want to go, list all the possible ways you can think of to get there. When you are doing this, be creative and try not to eliminate any of your ideas until you can't think of any more. You might even ask someone to "brainstorm" with you. This will help you generate a number of possible solutions quickly and also help you to look creatively at alternatives. When your list is done, it's time to decide on which path you are going to take and what steps will get you there. Commit to a course of action and don't put it off. Remember, the worst that can happen is that your solution won't work. But if you don't try, you'll definitely stay stuck. Finally, give yourself tons of credit for having gone through this process! And, no matter what the outcome, you are building confidence in yourself as a problem-solver for the next time.

* * *

As you get older, decisions you have to make are not only tougher but have more long-term consequences. So, it is very important to learn some strategies for decision making and problem solving. One strategy is to make a list of all the pros and cons or possible solutions to a problem. This way, you can see in black and white what the choices are. It can be very helpful to go over your list with a friend or trusted adult. They may have some ideas you just didn't think of. After you've got your ideas all down on paper, put a star next to the ones that seem to be more important, or the best solutions. This will help you get a clearer sense of direction. Another strategy is to break the problem down into small steps. Every big problem is made up of lots of baby steps, and if you break down the big problem into manageable pieces, it will feel much more doable. But remember, if the answer was easy, you would have thought of it right away. Most decisions have a number of pros and cons, and most problems have more than one solution. The task is to find the decision or solution that is right for you.

Why is money more important to some people than happiness? *Eliza, age 17*

Very few people would admit to putting money before happiness, yet many people behave as if money is the most important thing in their lives. We live in a culture where accumulating things like cars, houses, clothes, trips, and status has become a measure of "success." People will claim that these things are enjoyable in their own right, and they make them feel important and secure. If you ask the average person what makes them happy, they will usually talk about love, their family, their work, contributing to the community, and financial security. Accumulating wealth often comes last on their list of values. However, for a lot of people, their behavior tells us that the pursuit of money is very important, because, in actuality, they spend more time making it and spending it than they do with their families, loved ones, or hobbies. In truth, happiness and money are very intertwined. Money makes people happy because of what it can bring to them in terms of things, security, and status. All people, teenagers and adults alike, can benefit from looking at their values about money and happiness, in order to see whether what they are doing with their money is truly making them happy. Take some time to think about what really makes you happy. You can even make a list. If you're honest, you'll see that being loved, valued, and wanted by people you care about is just as important, or even more important, than having money or loads of things. Realizing this in your teen years, and not forgetting it, will go a long way in making you a happier adult.

Why do adolescents tend to put so much importance on material things and money?
Molly, age 16

We are a society that, rightly or wrongly, puts a tremendous emphasis on material things and money. Adolescence is often a very insecure, awkward time when teens are trying to figure out questions like "Who am I?" and "How do I get other kids to like me?" Owning "things," such as the "right" kind of sneakers or clothes from the "right" store, often gives kids positive recognition from their peers or reassures them that they won't be teased or put down. Having material things helps make some people feel more adequate. This is true not just for teens but for many adults too. It is important to remember that what another person has doesn't really tell us very much about who she or he is as a person. As you get older, although material things will continue to be important, you will find out that it is the quality of people that is most important, not what they own. During your teen years, clothes and possessions are important tools to help you explore your identity. The idea is to not let them *become your identity*.

* * *

Adolescence is usually the first time in your life when you have "discretionary money," that is, money you can spend on whatever you want. Businesses that market products to teens spend billions of dollars a year on advertising to create a desire for their products. You're literally bombarded with hundreds of messages over the course of a week about what you "need" to be a successful, popular person. You have to have a certain look. You are told you need to buy, wear, or use particular products. So, it is not surprising that a good part of the importance teens place on material things comes from being influenced by advertisements that tell teens what they need to be popular and successful. At the same time, you are learning how to develop an image for yourself and usually want to use your money to buy products that shape your image. Welcome to consumerism! While having the power (money) to buy certain things feels good for everyone, be careful that you don't start thinking that simply having the "right stuff" will make you happy. Being happy comes from how you feel inside —the "stuff" is just the icing on the cake.

Why should I start organizing money?
Erika, age 13

You should start organizing your money because learning to manage money is one of the more important life tasks you will have to master. Organizing money means being able to budget, spend, and save according to a plan. The same skills that are necessary for organizing money can also help you organize your time and priorities (what is important to you). Part of organizing money is developing the self-discipline to live within the budget you plan for yourself, and lots of adults don't do this very well. You have to learn to delay buying something sometimes. On the other hand, there are occasionally times when you really want something and you decide to borrow money to get what you absolutely "must have." If you do this, you should also have a plan about how you are going to pay it back. These are tough decisions. It is definitely better to get started learning how to make these choices now, and not wait until later on, when they will be more complicated and difficult.

* * *

Just like other things, the good habits you start now will pay off later. When parents and other adults talk with teens about learning to manage things like their money and their time, they often make them feel like this is a skill they are just supposed to have. They are wrong. Managing money and time are not skills you are born with. They have to be learned, and it is much harder than it seems. Here are some ideas to get you started:

- Figure out how much money you earn each week. It may come from a job, like babysitting, from an allowance, or from income you get for doing chores around your house.
- List each of these on a piece of paper under the heading "Income." Then add them all up, and you will see how much you have coming in each week.
- Now list your expenses (things you buy that your parents don't pay for). You might like to buy an extra soda or a snack at school each day. How much do you spend going out on weekends? Whatever your expenses are, list them under the heading "Expenses." Now add these up.
- Look at the difference between your income and your expenses. If your expenses are greater than your income, you probably owe money to one or more people, and you need to think about ways to earn more or spend less.
- If your income is greater than your expenses, you've probably got a stash, so that when something comes up, you have the funds for it. Good for you!

Keeping a budget and staying out of debt is a habit that will make you feel less stressed about money now and as you grow up.

Why won't businesses give teens a chance when they are looking for employment? They say, "You don't have enough experience." But I never will if no one gives me a first chance.
Mary, age 17

It doesn't make sense, does it? No matter how unfair this is, it is a reality of the job market. Putting energy into being disgruntled, discouraged, or angry simply won't help you. Instead, use your energy to think of how to convince an employer that you are really worth hiring. What do *you* have to offer a potential employer that would make her or him want to take a chance on you, despite your lack of experience? Are you enthusiastic, eager to learn, flexible? Are you a hard worker? Do you have a positive attitude? Sell yourself on your strengths. If you don't get a particular job, don't take it personally. If you're confident in your ability to learn and to perform well on the job, you will find an employer who will take a chance on you. It may take many interviews or applications, but you need only one "yes" to land a job. Sometimes, being willing to volunteer on a job can give you the experience you need to land a paying job. If you stick with it and stay positive, you are bound to get that first job.

Hot Tips

☞ Learn to manage your money now. You'll avoid a big source of stress later on in life!

☞ Finding that first job can be tough, especially if you don't have any experience. Talk to friends who have a job—they can help you with how to find one and what to expect. *Sell* your enthusiasm, your willingness to learn, and your sense of responsibility to potential employers.

☞ There are far too many demands on teens today. Sometimes there's not enough time in the day to get everything done. Set priorities, make sure you do the things that are really important to you and don't be upset if *everything* can't get done.

☞ If your life seems chaotic and disorganized, don't panic. Make lists of the things you have to do. Put all your appointments on a calendar. Reward yourself for accomplishing things on your list and keeping your appointments. You can do it!

☞ It's really hard to stick to a schedule, especially if it's one that someone else has made for you. Try taking control of your life by making your own *realistic* schedule. You're more likely to stick to a schedule that *you* make.

☞ Some kids have lots of "stuff," like expensive clothes, a car, or lots of money to spend. Sure you feel jealous. But remember, stuff alone won't make you happy.

☞ One of the best ways to solve problems or make decisions is to make a list of the pros and cons and the possible solutions. Then you can see all the choices and issues at once. It really helps.

7

Are All Families This Difficult to Live With?

My parents are on my case all the time. I can't stand the pressure. My brother has it so easy—he gets all the privileges, and I have tons of rules. Ever since my parents got divorced, my mother has been so much stricter. I bet my stepfather keeps telling her that I'm spoiled. And what's worse is that my parents don't trust me to do anything. They're so overprotective. I just can't stand it.—*Lydia*

My parents put a lot of pressure on me. What should I do? *Claudette, age 16*

If your parents are putting a lot of pressure on you, you probably feel angry, anxious, worried, or sad. Start by letting your parents know how you are feeling. Tell them you need to talk with them and agree on a good time to do this. Pick a time when things aren't too busy or hectic. Let them know you are feeling pressured, and give them examples of what they are doing and how it makes you feel. For example, you might say, "When you tell me that I need to stay home and do extra work because it is the only way I'll stay out of trouble and get into college, it makes me feel stressed and upset. I know it's important that I do well in school and stay safe, but I also need to have a life and to have more time with my friends." Let your parents know that you understand they just want what is best for you, and suggest better ways they can support you, like, "How about if I can have Friday nights and Saturday afternoons with my friends, then on Sundays I'll stay home and get all my chores and homework done."

Sometimes it is also helpful to talk with others you trust, like friends, teachers, school counselors, someone from church, or another adult in your extended family (like a grandparent, aunt, or uncle). Believe it or not, just talking about the pressures can help relieve them!

* * *

Parents put pressure on teens for lots of different reasons. When it comes to school, your parents want you to succeed, and they believe that hard work and lots of studying will result in success. Your parents might also pressure you to live your life in certain ways—for instance, to dress in certain ways, to have certain friends, to go out for certain sports or activities. They may also have expectations for you to work and help around the house. Handling schoolwork, friends, household chores, working after school, and helping take care of younger siblings all can make teens feel pressured and really stressed out.

The first thing to do is to figure out what your "pressure points" are. Make a list of pressure points, and divide it into school, friends, home, and outside activities. Remember, if you've got more going on than any one human being can handle, you're going to feel pressured all the time. Your list can help you figure out how much your parents are actually pressuring you or if your whole life is just one big pressure cooker. Then, if you still feel like the greatest source of pressure is your parents, talk to them. Let them know how they are pressuring you. Try to listen to your parents' reasons for being on your case, even if you don't agree with them. Let them know that you have listened to them and can understand and appreciate their point of view. Tell them that, since *you* are trying to understand their point of view, it is important that *they* understand yours, too. Make every effort to reach some compromise so that both their concerns and yours are considered.

* * *

Your parents' backgrounds, including where and how they were raised, influence the way they treat you. For example, parents who come from poor families may put pressure on their children to work and save money, or parents who were raised by strict parents may have more trouble giving their kids freedom. For parents, their children's success is a measure of their success. One way to get your parents to cool down is to show them how responsible you are. You can do this by completing your homework, doing your chores, and keeping your curfew. Having a teacher put a comment on your report card that you have missed assignments is asking for trouble! The more you show your parents how responsible you are, the greater the chance that they will ease up on you. This will also help your parents to believe that you are capable of making good decisions about important things in your life.

Another way to get your parents to ease up is to tell them how you plan to meet your responsibilities. For example, you can say, "Please don't remind me about my homework, and I promise to get it done by 10 p.m. every night if you don't bug me." If you keep your part of the bargain, you'll have some ammunition to persuade them to keep theirs.

Why do teens disagree with their parents on so many topics? *Meagan, age 14*

First of all, it's totally normal for you to disagree with your parents! Like most teens, you are discovering who you are by spending more and more time with your friends, surfing the Internet, reading e-mails, going to movies, choosing your own clothes, and listening to music. This is how most teens develop and express their individuality and their own opinions. It is what we call *autonomy*. You are becoming more self-reliant.

But, as you probably know, doing things on your own and forming your own opinions can lead to conflict between you and your parents. When disagreements are about house rules, sometimes you can compromise. However, at other times, your parents may feel very strongly about certain rules, which they are not about to change. It is important for you and your parents to listen to each other and try to understand the reasons behind each of your views. Perhaps you will not come to an agreement, but you and your parents *can agree to disagree*. One of the unfortunate facts about not being on your own yet is that you cannot be your own boss all of the time. You cannot have all the power you want! But this does not mean that you can't hold on to your own opinions, even though you may have to follow their rules.

* * *

It is natural for teens to disagree with their parents and to want to become more and more separate and independent. This is the time in your life when you want to make your own decisions, rather than having your parents make all your decisions for you. At the same time, your body is changing, and there is a lot for you to get used to. You may feel pressure to look a certain way, to dress in certain clothes, to have sex, or to use drugs and alcohol. The kinds of pressures you face may be different depending on your age, race, and culture and the neighborhood, town, or city you live in. It's normal for your parents to worry about all the changes you are going through.

Why do they worry so much? As unfair as it may be, many parents feel that teenage girls are more likely to get hurt or get into trouble than boys. Your parents might also be upset that you don't want to be at home as much anymore and want to have your own private life. Maybe your parents dislike your taste in clothes, music, or movies. What can you do?

You might try this. Ask your parents to make a list of the things they think you and they agree about and the things you disagree about. At the same time, you make your own list. Use your lists to acknowledge your differences and, more importantly, to see where you agree. Make an effort to focus on the "agrees" rather than the "disagrees." You might be surprised to find that there is more that you agree about than you originally thought.

* * *

It is your job to disagree with your parents! Your teen years are the time in your life when you are trying to establish who you are as a separate and unique person from your parents. If you accepted all your parents' ideas without question, then you would never develop a clear idea about what *you* think. But there are lots of ways of expressing your different views to your parents. Words are your best tool for communicating with them. It is right and necessary for you to want to voice what you think and feel because it is your way of expressing who you are. If you can't seem to get your parents to listen by talking to them, try writing or sending them an e-mail. Sometimes parents listen better when they have time to think about what you have to say.

What do you do with overprotective parents? *Jennifer, age 13*

Parents overprotect their children because they love them and are afraid that something bad could happen to them. Many parents believe that the world you are growing up in is more dangerous than it was when they were growing up. At the same time, most teens don't think about bad things happening to them until they actually experience it. For example, if someone you know has been hurt or killed because they were in a car with a drunk driver, you are probably more understanding of your parents' fears than you would be if this has never happened to you.

If you think your parents are unreasonably overprotective, you can demonstrate that you are capable of taking care of yourself by letting them see you be responsible with your possessions, schoolwork, siblings, friends, and chores. This will allow them to see that you are growing up and need less protection than you did before. Give them a chance to tell you what they think is important for you to be an independent and responsible person. Then you can work on com-

ing to an agreement together about things like curfews and dating.

* * *

The teen years can be a hard time because parents
and kids often disagree about how much freedom and
independence teens can handle responsibly and safely.
In your mind, there are probably a whole bunch of
things you feel you could handle on your own that
your parents interfere with. And, your parents are
probably thinking about all the dangers in the world
that could hurt their daughter! This may seem unfair,
but the reality is that it happens a lot with teens your
age.

Try starting a conversation with your parents.
First, tell them you understand their point of view.
Let them know you understand some of the reasons
why they would want to protect you. This is very
important because it sets the stage for your parents to
feel like you understand their concerns and fears.
Then point out that for you to grow more competent
and mature, you need increased independence. Independence allows kids to practice new skills, develop
self-confidence, and prove their trustworthiness. Tell
them you want more freedom for these reasons. Now
here's the most important thing. Parents place a great
deal of importance on having their daughters grow up
to be strong and competent. It's right up there in
importance with protecting you! So, if you talk to
your parents about strengths you want to develop, instead of just your desire to "get out on your own,"

they may be more willing to support your having more independence.

* * *

Your parents must feel that there are things they need to protect you from. Instead of just arguing about what you want, begin by asking them what exactly they are afraid of. Then, think about what they have said. Ask yourself if you honestly believe their fears are realistic. Even if you don't think all of them are realistic, the best way to get them to be less protective is to ask them for a chance to show that you can make responsible and safe decisions for yourself about *some* things. Show them that you are willing to ask them for help if you're not sure what to do. In other words, let them know that you value their advice and guidance. This shows your maturity and thoughtfulness. While you can definitely battle it out with them, working with them, rather than against them, will get you better results. If you let them in on some of your life, they will worry less about the rest. But don't forget, if they give in even a little, and then you blow it, you're back to where you started.

Is there a way to deal with favoritism from your parents toward another sibling?
Rebecca, age 15

Many kids feel their parents favor a sibling because they believe that they buy more stuff for him or her, spend more time with him or her, give him or her more attention, or take his or her side in arguments. Sometimes, you might be right! Your sister or brother might be getting more than you! When you feel this kind of favoritism is happening in your family, you might consider the possibility that there are reasons your parents are behaving this way. Maybe your mom is buying your sister more things because she is going away to college and needs certain things at this time. Perhaps your little brother gets more attention than you because he acts out more and needs more discipline. Maybe your parents are helping your brother or sister more with homework because he or she needs extra help to get good grades when you do well with less help. This is sort of a compliment when you think about it.

When things are lopsided, it is natural to feel left out and hurt, but silence is not the answer. If you feel you would like your parents to spend more time with you, think about what you would like to do with them and then ask them to plan a time to do it. This will work much better than making angry accusations or yelling something like "You never take me anywhere or do anything with me!"

* * *

Feeling "unfavored" usually means feeling unhappy, overlooked, invisible, and unworthy. However, most of the time the sibling being favored and the parent who is doing the favoring don't have a clue about how you feel. You are the only one feeling bad in this situation. First, there are a few things you should not do:

1. Don't commit drastic actions to get noticed. Your parents won't get it, and this could make matters worse.
2. Don't believe you deserve to be "unfavored." It will only make *you* unhappy, not anyone else.
3. Don't compete.

Now, the things you should do are

1. Remind yourself of all your good qualities, like your ability to make others laugh, play sports, play music or sing, be a good friend, or do well in math.
2. Find your own place in the sun. Do what you like to do because you love doing it, not to impress anyone else.
3. Don't let yourself get defeated. Pursue what you are good at, and shine in your own way.

Why do parents treat girls differently than boys? *Trisha, age 14*

In some families, boys have later curfews than girls (or no curfews at all), can date at a younger age, or have different responsibilities around the house. The truth of the matter is, women and girls in our society are treated differently than men and boys. As unfair as it is, there is also a realistic side. Being a girl makes you strong in a lot of ways but also vulnerable in other ways. For example, girls are more likely to be victims of certain crimes, such as being mugged or sexually abused. Your parents worry about these things and want you to be safe.

Talk to your parents if you feel they are treating you differently, and explain to them why you think things may not be equal or fair. For example, you can say, "My curfew is 10:00 and Keith's was 12:00 when he was my age." Listen to your parents' reasoning, and then try to compromise. For example, suggest that your curfew be at 11:00 and that you will let them know where you are and whom you're with.

* * *

Parents aren't the only ones who treat girls differently than boys. Teachers, coaches, relatives, and all of society treat girls differently than boys. Some of the reasons are not acceptable and therefore unjust. But there are some valid differences between boys and girls that parents, teachers, and you have to pay attention to, even if you feel it's unfair. For example, girls are more at risk for developing eating disorders than boys are. Girls are also more likely than boys to experience depression. Girls are more affected by the consequences of sexual activity (like pregnancy and parenthood) than boys are. Girls are more often victims of physical or sexual abuse.

Parents cannot ignore these risks and often set rules to protect their daughters. Take some time to stop and think honestly about whether your parents' rules are realistic or truly unfair. Letting them know that you can see why some of their rules are different for you and your brother will help them to see that you understand that some of the dangers girls face are different than the ones boys face.

Is it common for lots of problems to arise between an adolescent and their parents when there's a stepparent involved? *Sarah, age 15*

The simple answer to your question is yes, problems often arise in your relationship with a parent when a stepparent enters the picture. But remember that if a stepparent has joined your family, everyone in your family has to adjust, not just you! This can be pretty hard.

Let's take a closer look at what happens when a new member joins a family. Before your stepparent was around, you and your parent probably had a pretty good understanding of each other and knew what to expect from one another. A stepparent will change this. You and your parent will have to change your relationship a little to make room for the new person in your lives. However, while your mother or father wants this new partner, you may not! At times, you are going to feel hurt, angry, or jealous that you have to share your parent's time, energy, and emotional life with another person. In addition, you may not like your new stepparent. There is no rule that says you have to like anyone! But figuring out how to get along with your stepparent will definitely make your life easier.

And remember, many stepparents are very nervous about how to relate to their new partner's children. You can help them out by letting them know what you would like them to do and how you would like to be treated. For example, it is better to tell your new stepparent that you need some time and space to get used to him or her rather than ignoring him or her or being hostile and angry and finding fault with everything he or she does. The key is to remember that these changes in your life can be hard. While your needs and desires are definitely important, so are the needs and desires of everyone involved.

* * *

Problems often occur between parents and their teens when a stepparent becomes part of the family. You might feel that your mother or father is not spending as much time with you as before. It can also be tough because your stepparent is just getting to know you and wasn't around when you were younger. So, you may resent when they do things like set rules or try to get close to you too quickly. What's more, if your mother, father, and stepparent don't get along, or disagree about things like your responsibilities, curfews, or money, you can feel pulled between all these adults. This will really make you feel stressed out.

When this happens to you, sit down and think about or make a list of what is upsetting you about all the changes in your family. Think about how these changes are making you feel. Then, talk to your parent and stepparent. You may decide you feel more comfortable talking with your parent first and then talking with your parent and stepparent together. Try to remember to be calm, honest, and respectful. Voicing what you think and how you feel can help smooth things out and make everyone feel better. And remember, adjusting to change always takes time.

Why do I feel that it was my fault that my mother and father got divorced? How do I handle being stuck in the middle? *Vanessa, age 16*

It is not unusual for kids to feel some responsibility for their parents' divorce. Sometimes, because they are angry or hurt themselves, parents might directly or indirectly give their kids the feeling that the divorce is their fault. If this has happened to you, remember that *it is not your fault!* Parents make the decision to divorce because they cannot work out their differences. But these problems are theirs and not yours. Try to keep telling yourself "It is not my fault."

You may be so mad at both of your parents for not being able to work things out and stay together that your anger scares you. Sometimes your anger might be so scary that you wind up blaming yourself rather than your parents. Often, when we feel pain and hurt, we look for someone to blame. It's human nature. It can help if you ask yourself some questions. Are you being the hero and taking the blame? If you are, it is not yours to take. Your parents made the decision to divorce, not you. So, what can you do? Try talking with the parent you feel will listen the best. If neither parent is willing to listen, find another adult you trust, like a relative or friend. Sometimes talking to a professional counselor or therapist is necessary to help you and your parents get through this very difficult time.

* * *

When parents divorce, many kids end up feeling like it may have been their fault. While you may *feel* responsible for the divorce, you *are not* responsible for the decisions your parents have made about their relationship. However, even if you know this, you might still end up feeling guilty.

So, let's look at some reasons why you still may be feeling guilty. You may believe, deep down, that your feelings of anger or hatred toward one or both of your parents caused them to break up. You may even have wished that your parents would break up at one point. Or, you may believe that your "bad behavior" caused them to fight all the time or was too much for one or the other of your parents to handle. If you believe this, you are not giving your parents credit for decisions they make about each other. In other words, you are putting yourself in the middle of a situation that affects you in a big way but is really between your parents.

Maybe one of your parents, or someone else in the family, said to you in anger, "You caused this!" It's like someone saying that you caused someone to have a heart attack or stroke. You caused *nothing*. If you feel stuck in the middle, tell your parents that you will not deliver a message from one to the other, that you will not spy on one parent for the other, that you will not take sides when they are arguing, and that you refuse to listen to one of them put down or bad-mouth the other. You have an absolute right to stay out of the middle. Remember that the person in the middle takes the most heat because they are taking it from both sides. Give yourself a break and stay out of it, even if one or the other parent labels you as "disloyal" or "disinterested."

* * *

It's normal for you to want to make things better in your family. You love your parents and want your family to stay together. You feel sadness and pain because your family can't all live together. Even though one or both of your parents may seem overwhelmed with their own feelings, it is important that you tell them how you feel, and it is also important that you seek out someone you can trust outside your immediate family (like an aunt, family friend, or counselor) who you can talk with. Divorce can feel lonely. Connecting with friends who you feel will understand what you're going through and will be willing to support you is very important.

When you feel stuck in the middle, try letting

your parents know that this makes you feel very uncomfortable. Perhaps you can agree to a signal ahead of time to let them know you are getting stuck in the middle again. Make up a "time-out" or other creative signal. It will be a great relief to you if you can help each of your parents to respect your special relationship with the other parent, regardless of the conflicts or disagreements they may have between them.

Hot Tips

☞ Let your parents know that pressuring you only makes you feel more stressed out. Show your parents that you are on top of things. This will go a long way toward calming them down.

☞ It's normal to disagree with your parents. You're growing up in a different time and in a different world. Be patient and try to imagine how tough it is for them to understand your world.

☞ It's a fact: Girls are treated differently than boys. Sometimes there are good reasons for this, and sometimes you are being treated unfairly for no reason. Be mature enough to listen to the reasons your parents give, and accept those that make sense.

☞ It's hard to adjust to parents divorcing. Remember, big life changes take time to get used to. Don't let your divorced parents put you in the middle.

☞ Give a new stepparent a chance. He or she is also adjusting to living with you.

☞ Do you feel like your parents favor your sister or brother? Or is it that your sibling *needs* more time or attention than you do? If you are feeling ignored, ask for some time. Don't just sit and stew about it.

8

Eating Disorders, Anxiety, Depression: How Can I Tell If I'm Really in Trouble?

Some of my friends are so messed up. My friend Abby is depressed all the time. She secretly told me that she thinks about killing herself. I want to tell someone, but she made me promise not to. I don't know what to do. I'm pretty sure my other friend Alexandra has an eating disorder. She's constantly talking about how many calories something has, and all she eats is lettuce! I try to be there for them, but I've got so much of my own stuff to deal with. I feel anxious and stressed all the time. I don't know what to do.—*Lauren*

What causes mood swings? *Martha, age 15*

During the teen years, mood swings are caused by both physical and psychological changes. Normal adolescence is accompanied by physical changes such as rapid growth, hormonal increases, and biochemical changes in the brain that affect your mood. Psychological factors include increased sensitivity to criticism, concerns about relationships and friendships, and worries about being able to be successful in school and in your future life.

We still don't know exactly how these physical and psychological factors interact to create mood swings. Nevertheless, when a negative mood persists over a long time, our view of the world may become quite bleak. When this happens, you may experience negative thoughts about yourself or feelings of helplessness and hopelessness about the future. You may also have some physical signs, like headaches or upset stomachs. On the other hand, there may be times when you feel so "up" and energized that you want to do everything. At these times, you might find yourself running from one thing to another so quickly that your friends may say, "Boy, are you wired." Either way, mood swings are a normal part of adolescence. It is only when they are constantly extreme and last a long time that there might be a serious problem. If your mood swings start to interfere with your life, talk to your parents. It's probably time to get professional help.

* * *

Mood swings or rapidly changing feelings sometimes happen for no apparent reason and are common among adolescents. For example, you might wake up feeling fine in the morning and then become confused by your feelings of sadness in the afternoon. You might get angry and annoyed too easily and fly off the handle. Changes in your mood are connected with the many physical changes that are going on in your body (like changes in hormones) and with the different challenges you now face (like increased schoolwork). How you see your body and your increased sensitivity to how others respond to you might make you even more moody.

How can I deal with depression and depressed friends? *Linda, age 13*

If you are feeling depressed, the first thing to do is to find someone who will listen without trying to tell you that you should not feel so sad or that you have nothing to worry about. Your concerns are serious and real. If a friend wants to talk to you about being depressed, the same is true. The role of listener is very important—just listening without trying to fix the situation is helpful. But it is also important to remember that depression can be very serious. It can be much deeper than the sadness everyone feels now and again. This kind of depression may need the help of a professional. If you fear for the safety of someone who has confided in you, talk to an adult you trust right away, and get help as quickly as possible.

* * *

There are different kinds of depression. The most common is "having the blues" or feeling down. This kind of depressed feeling follows experiencing a loss. The loss can be something physical, like losing a favorite tape or jacket. It can also be a psychological loss, like not feeling good about yourself because someone snubs you in school. Or maybe you had a fight at home and feel bad about it. Maybe you're feeling discriminated against. Maybe you flunked an important test.

This kind of depression is a "people problem." Something is not working in an important relationship in your life. Just moping and keeping it to yourself probably won't work. There are two different paths you can take to feel better. First, if you can, go directly to the person you are having a problem with and talk it through. Once you figure out what isn't working in that relationship, it will be easier to fix it. However, if you can't go directly to that person, the other path might work better for you. This path involves finding a way to feel better about yourself before you work on fixing the people problem. Start by talking to someone you trust, like a friend, parent, or counselor. Tell him or her that you feel down. At the time, even if you don't feel like it, push yourself to be active. Physical activity causes chemical changes in your body that improve your mood. Once you are feeling better, you can decide whether you want to go back to the first path and address the people problem directly or just let it go.

If it is a friend who is feeling down, here are a couple of tips. Encourage your friend to talk to you and tell you what is going on. Then you can use a technique called *reflective listening*. This involves letting the person know you really heard and understood how they feel. Say things like, "That really sucks!" or "You feel hurt that he didn't talk to you," or "You're really mad that your mother doesn't understand you." The more your friend feels understood, the faster her blues will lift. Try not to offer advice (this is a tough one!) about what to do. Instead, encourage your friend to think about solutions she can put into place. While the depressed feelings might be uncomfortable, feeling blue is a natural part of life. Being there for a friend, and asking a friend to be there for you, is the best way to beat the blues.

Some forms of depression are much more serious. "Clinical depression" is different than just having the blues. The symptoms include difficulty sleeping or sleeping longer than you normally sleep, a change in appetite where you eat more or less than you usually do, a loss of energy, and not being able to experience pleasure in the things you used to enjoy. Very depressed people may also have thoughts of killing themselves. While everyone has one or more of these symptoms at one time or another, the time to be concerned is if any of the symptoms lasts more than a few weeks or if the feeling is very intense. If you or your friend have thoughts of hurting yourself, the time to get professional help is *now*.

How can I deal with my anxiety? *Grace, age 18*

Anxiety, or feelings of stress and tension, tend to increase during the teen years. How to deal with these feelings depends on what situations you tend to feel anxious in and how intense the feelings of anxiety are. For example, it is not uncommon for people to feel anxious when they are going to take a test, give a talk in front of a group of people, or go on an interview for school or a job. However, these feelings of anxiety typically do not make it impossible for the person to actually take the test, talk in front of the group, or go on the interview. Usually these feelings of anxiety go away after the person has completed the activity. While it is natural to try to avoid situations that make you feel anxious, it is better to learn how to cope effectively with your anxiety.

Anxiety isn't just an emotional feeling; it's also physical. Anxiety can show itself in your body through an increase in your heart rate, muscle tightening, sweating palms, and shortness of breath. So, it is a good idea to practice relaxing before you are in a situation that makes you anxious. Once you are good at this, you can do it more easily when you need it.

Here's what to do: Find a quiet place, turn down the lights, and think about a calm situation, like when you were relaxing on the beach or by a pool. When you get anxious, picture this image, and let the calm feeling take over. After all, you can't be calm and anxious at the same time. Right before starting something that makes you anxious (like speaking in front of a class), close your eyes and picture your calming scene. Here are some other examples of relaxing activities that can help you to calm down, either before or after an anxious situation: listen to music, read, pray, take a hot bath or shower, exercise, or talk it out with a friend.

For some people, feelings of anxiety become so strong that they feel they can't cope—these people can't take the test, speak in front of the group, or go on the interview. Their anxiety interferes with their everyday activities. If you can't deal with your anxiety using calming or relaxing techniques, and your anxiety continues to make you unable to participate in everyday activities, you should consider getting some professional help.

* * *

There are several "tools" that can help you deal with anxiety. One of them is learning how to breathe from your diaphragm, slowly and deeply. Breathing is important because it determines the amount of tension that we feel. Because we all start out in life breathing the "right" way, you may just need to reteach yourself how to do it, or you may want to get some help, for instance from your music teacher or gym teacher. Put your hand on your stomach, and make sure that your "belly" acts like a balloon when you breathe, going *out* when you inhale and going *in* when you exhale. Learn to inhale to a count of four and exhale to a count of four.

Another tool for dealing with your anxiety is to "plan when to be anxious": Set aside a half hour every day to think about the things that worry you. But there are two rules: You have to stop at the end of the half hour, and you have to make the time to do the same thing the next day. That way, if you find yourself anxious later on, you can tell yourself, "I'll deal with this during my planned time to be anxious."

A third tool for dealing with anxiety is problem solving. This technique can help you focus and learn more about yourself. Get a paper and pencil, and write down your answers to the following questions: What am I anxious about? Under what circumstances? When does it start? What makes it better or worse? How long does it last? And what makes it go away? You'll be surprised at how much better you can deal with your anxiety when you are clearer about your answers to these questions.

* * *

Anxiety is a powerful feeling that can sometimes overwhelm us. When we are anxious, we sometimes feel restless and irritable and get tired more easily. We feel muscle tension, maybe we can't sleep well, and we have a hard time concentrating, too. Some people use food to distract themselves. Food can be soothing and make you feel better for a little while, but you need to find out what is making you so anxious, because "quick fixes," like food, don't last. Start by asking yourself, "What causes my anxiety?" Is it something about yourself, your relationships with other people (friends, parents, boyfriend), schoolwork?

Once you know something about what is causing your anxiety, you can focus on controlling it. For example, if you are worried about your schoolwork, instead of just stewing, you can decrease your anxiety by taking some action: You might make appointments to meet with your teachers to talk about how you are doing and find out ways to improve. A step-by-step action plan will lower your anxiety.

How do I know whether or not I have an eating disorder? *Denise, age 16*

There are several types of eating disorders. You may have heard about anorexia or bulimia. Anorexia is a serious eating disorder in which a person does not eat the amount and variety of foods that her body needs to stay healthy, and she gets thinner and thinner but remains concerned that she is still too fat. While bulimia is similar to anorexia in that the person is worried about her weight no matter how thin she is, bulimia usually involves binge eating (eating very large amounts of food at one time) and taking laxatives or throwing up (purging) to get rid of the food. Overeating is another eating disorder and, like anorexia and bulimia, it is a way of avoiding dealing with difficult thoughts and feelings instead of working them through directly. All eating disorders are dangerous, and sometimes a person doesn't even know she is really hurting herself.

So, if you even only *think* you have a problem, talk to someone right away. Your pediatrician, school counselor, dietician, and psychologist are the best people to ask about eating disorders. It's good to ask an expert because eating disorders can really mess up your body and your head. Because each person is different, you really have to talk to someone directly to know if you have this problem.

* * *

Several thoughts and feelings typically go along with eating disorders. These include spending a lot of time thinking about food, being preoccupied with eating or not eating something, worrying about allowing yourself to eat, and constantly thinking about what you don't like about your body. While most teens are concerned about how they look, those with eating disorders think about food and their bodies all the time. Do thoughts about food and eating interfere with your life? Do they affect your schoolwork, friendships, ability to play sports, or other interests and activities? Has anyone expressed concern to you about your eating or your weight? Each of these may be a sign that you have a problem.

As women in this culture, we are brought up to think that how our bodies look is a major indication of our value, both in terms of ability and attractiveness. For this reason, many girls and women spend a fair amount of time thinking about eating, food, and how they look. This becomes a problem when it interferes with our life, changes how we feel about ourselves, or results in having unhealthy eating habits. It's also a problem if you think that what you eat and how you look will solve all your other problems. Disordered eating, even if it doesn't have a fancy name of an eating disorder, is a real problem and can lead to serious health problems.

* * *

We all worry about food sometimes and either overeat or skip a meal on occasion. But, if you have an eating disorder, you worry about food for many hours each day and may think about food and eating in peculiar ways. Ask yourself a few questions:

- Are you satisfied with your body?
- Are you always on a diet?
- Do you often eat large amounts of food, eat rapidly, and feel out of control when you eat?
- Have you ever vomited or spit out food after feeling like you ate too much?
- Do you overexercise when you feel you ate too much?
- Do you skip meals or restrict food intake for fear of weight gain?
- Do you spend a lot of your time thinking about food, weight, or eating?
- Do you see your clothes size as a measure of your value as a person?
- Do you use food to distract yourself from feelings

such as anger, rejection, frustration, boredom, or loneliness?

- Do you "feel fat" even when others tell you that you are thin?

If your answer to more than one of these questions is "yes," you could be on the road to an eating disorder. Tell someone about how you are feeling and get help. You *can* learn to manage difficult feelings and feel good about your body.

How do you help anorexic friends?
Carlotta, age 15

It's tough to help a friend who has anorexia. While you may be worried and afraid for her, she may not seem worried about herself. In fact, many times girls who have anorexia tell their friends "I do not have a problem." But anorexia can be fatal. Your friend needs help. Be supportive and let her know you care about her, but don't pressure her to eat because it won't work. Instead, encourage her to talk to you about herself—about what she is thinking and how she is feeling. While at first she may have trouble opening up, if you keep asking and talking, she will probably become more open with you. It also helps to share some of your own struggles with your friend and to talk about how you handle your problems. When you talk to her, keep suggesting that getting professional help is really important. While she may resist in the beginning, don't stop trying. You can also try telling her about the dangers of anorexia, like the possibilities of heart failure, kidney failure, digestive problems, and electrolyte imbalance. While this information may not ring a bell with her immediately, later on if she reaches the point where she doesn't feel well, she might remember what you told her.

Above all, remember you can only do so much. In anorexia, girls come to falsely believe that the way to improve their self-worth is to have total control over their bodies by severely restricting what they eat. They do this because they don't feel in control of the rest of their lives. Your friend has to come to value herself and improve her life in ways other than starving herself. She has to learn to appreciate herself as a person, not just focus on how she looks or what she eats.

* * *

There is a great deal of emphasis in our culture for girls and women to be thin. People with anorexia are always striving to be thin, thinner, or the thinnest. So, just telling a friend that she is too thin probably won't do much good. While you may not be able to change her perception of herself, there are things you can do to try to help. You can bring up your concern at a time when neither of you are stressed out. It may be most helpful if you talk about ways in which changes in her behavior are affecting you, or you might share your caring and your worry. Instead of accusing her, you might say, "I've noticed recently that you don't seem very happy. We used to enjoy talking with each other at lunchtime and hanging out together. Lately, you seem worried and preoccupied. Is there any way I can help?" It is also important to encourage your friend to talk with an adult who can help: a parent, a counselor, a favorite teacher. At the same time, keep supporting your friend's other interests and activities. This will help your friend to think about herself and her achievements in ways that don't have to do with her weight.

What is the definition of an obsession? How can I tell if I'm obsessed with something? *Alyssa, age 17*

Obsessions are words, phrases, or sentences we repeat to ourselves over and over again, even if they are not useful. Obsessions seem automatic, or involuntary, like a habit you cannot break. Often times the repetitive thoughts are unrelated to the situations in which they happen. Some experts believe that obsessive thoughts happen when we are wishing to control a part of our lives that we cannot control. An example of an obsession might be worrying over and over again about how to get someone to like you— but there is no way to control someone else's approval of you. Sometimes, obsessive thoughts lead to compulsive behaviors (something you feel you absolutely have to do), like having to say certain words or counting numbers as if they have a magical ability to reduce your anxiety and worry. Give yourself this test:

- Do you think about something so much that it gets in the way of doing the other things that you have to do?
- How much time are you really spending thinking about this thing?
- Are you thinking about it more than two hours a day?
- Do you find it impossible to push the thoughts away?

If your answer is "yes" to any of these questions, you might have an obsession. Obsessive thinking does not solve problems. You need to get the obsessive thoughts out of your mind to get on with your life.

* * *

Obsessions are thoughts that you can't stop yourself from thinking. You think about them most or all of the time. The thoughts seem to invade everything. When you try to sleep, the thoughts are there. When you are out with friends, you don't focus on your friends or what you are doing, but instead you are preoccupied with the thoughts. You can't concentrate on anything else. When you try to focus on something else, the obsessive thoughts just keep interrupting. You simply cannot force the thoughts to disappear. This problem can be temporary, in which case the thoughts begin to fade as circumstances change. But the problem may last for weeks or months and may grow in intensity. Then your quality of life really begins to suffer. If this happens to you, talk to an adult who you know will listen and take you seriously. There is help available for people who have difficulty with obsessive thoughts.

Why do people have phobias? *Georgia, age 18*

Many professionals believe that fears and phobias are learned. Basically, we learn to be afraid of something because it becomes associated with something bad. For example, you might be terrified of dogs because when you were much younger, you saw a movie where a dog attacked a child. Now, even though you are so much older and "know" that all dogs are not attack dogs, the phobia still persists. In fact, it might grow stronger. You might even avoid walking down a certain street because you once saw a dog there without a leash.

Phobias are so powerful because of the fear and avoidance cycle that is created. First, you learn to be afraid of something. Then naturally, you avoid the thing you fear. Finally, avoiding that thing reinforces your fear (making it worse) and makes it more likely that you will avoid that thing in the future. So, you never give yourself the chance to conquer your fear. You are caught in a vicious cycle. It also makes it likely that you will start to avoid things that remind you of that thing, "generalizing" the fear to even more things. So the dog phobia can become a cat phobia, too. And then, soon enough, you could be afraid of all animals.

One of the best ways to deal with a phobia like this, especially one that is getting in your way, like being afraid of dogs when your boyfriend has a dog that he loves, is to work to beat your fear. You can do this in a step-by-step process. The fancy term for this is *systematic desensitization*, and it works! Start by looking at pictures of what you are afraid of, in this case, dogs. Keep looking at the pictures while you work on relaxing and telling yourself, "I don't need to be afraid." After you can look at pictures of your fear more calmly, find a way to approach your fear gradually, like reach out to pet your boyfriend's dog while he holds him tightly on a leash. Practice this at least 10 or 12 times, and then see if you can approach your fear in a more relaxed way. With most phobias, you can beat your fear if you take it slow and maintain your determination.

Why am I afraid to sleep in my own house alone? Where does fear of being alone come from? *MaryLou, age 18*

The fear of being alone is normal. All human beings have this fear. However, girls are allowed to express this fear more openly than boys. In our culture, it is considered acceptable for a girl to be fearful of staying alone. Boys can feel equally fearful, but it is not as acceptable for a boy to express such a fear. Boys learn to hide their fears better than girls do, and therefore girls often think that boys are more courageous. This is not necessarily true.

When we are infants, we learn whether the world is basically safe or dangerous (to be feared). We learn this through images, not words. Try to describe a hologram. Unless you have an extensive vocabulary and the gift of verbal expression, this is very hard to do. The same is true for trying to describe our initial impressions about the safety of the world. If you are afraid to be alone, and there is no reason for this fear, then it is possible that you perceive the world as a dangerous place. Once you become aware that this is the problem, you can then work on changing your view of the world. If awful things have happened to you in the past, then therapy would be the best avenue for developing a worldview that helps you feel safe and frees you from overwhelming fear.

* * *

Fears can come from previous scary experiences, or they may just come from our own overactive imaginations. Being afraid to sleep in your own house could result from your being unfamiliar with all of its night noises. It could mean that you are upset or anxious about something else, and you would rather be with someone. One thing to try is to have an evening ritual that helps you relax. This could include locking the doors, putting on soothing music, drinking a cup of hot tea, and turning off all but one light. Think up your own personal "relaxers," and write them down. Then, the next time you are alone and afraid, try some of the things on your list. You'll be surprised at how many good ideas you can come up with and how well they work.

Because I was molested when I was younger, does that mean I'll be messed up for life? *Lilliana, age 18*

Having experienced sexual abuse is very serious, but it does *not* mean that you are destined to be "messed up" for life. Sexual abuse might affect you differently at different times in your life. For example, you may think that you are completely over the experience and then, months or years later, be reminded of it by something and feel upset about it all over again. If you have not talked with anyone about being abused, it is very important to do so as soon as possible. You don't have to feel funny about bringing it up now even if it happened years ago, because the very fact that you are asking about it shows that it is affecting how you feel and act now.

There are several support groups for teens who have experienced sexual abuse. Check these out with your local mental health association, clinic, or doctor. Talking to others who have gone through a similar experience will not only help you feel less alone but will also give you new ideas about how to manage your feelings. The worst thing you can do is keep the secret inside of you or think the abuse was your fault. It is not your fault, no matter what!

* * *

Being molested as a kid doesn't necessarily mean that you will be messed up for life. To begin with, let's be clear about one thing: People who molest kids have *big* problems. Molestation can never be excused. It's also important for you to know that many kids have any number of potentially damaging experiences and make it through them in pretty good shape. Whether or not you are hurt by an experience depends in part on how you understand what happened to you and in part on whether or not there are caring adults to help you understand and digest the experience. So, while any kind of uninvited physical contact, especially sexual abuse, is just plain wrong, how you understand your experience and the sense you make of it can help protect you from being "messed up."

Is it normal to think about suicide? *Tyler, age 16*

As teens mature, their ability to think about life and death also matures. With better reasoning and thinking skills, teens may find themselves thinking "what would it be like to die" or "what would it be like to kill myself." These are very different from serious thoughts of death or recurrent feelings of hopelessness. If someone is planning or fantasizing about suicide, it usually means that they are experiencing such extreme and overwhelming feelings of despair that they feel that dying is the only way out.

Thoughts and feelings about suicide need to be taken *very seriously,* and getting help immediately is critical.

If you or a friend are thinking about or have plans for suicide, you should tell someone about it *immediately.* Go to your school counselor, a psychologist, or any other adult you can get a hold of. If it is a friend with the suicidal thoughts, and she won't go for help, offer to go with her. Tell your friend that suicide may seem like the only way out at the time, but that talking with someone about the situation will help relieve the immediate stress and help her find other solutions. If she still refuses, go alone and notify someone about the problem. Suicide is never the answer!

* * *

The answer is, "Yes, it is normal to think about suicide." Many teens have thought about killing themselves at one time or another. At these times, the problem at hand just seems too big, or the embarrassment too great, to live through. However, the suicidal thought usually passes rather quickly, and you can think of other ways of managing the problem or the embarrassment. But, you need to seek help if the thought won't go away. You need to seek help immediately if you have a plan for killing yourself or the means to put the plan into action.

How should teenagers with all these emotional feelings discuss them with their parents, or should they? *Nora, age 16*

It's always a good idea to try to talk about your feelings with your parents. While this is not often easy, remember that when we don't talk about our feelings, they often show up in our behavior anyway. If you have a pretty open relationship with your parents, you will be able to talk about your feelings and your behaviors. Sometimes parents have trouble hearing about your feelings because they still want you to be their "little girl" and for you to have "problems" that they can easily solve. But, now that you are a teenager, your problems are often very complicated, and sometimes you want your parents to just listen and not try to figure out a solution. If you only want your parents to listen, tell them up front "I would like it if you would just listen to me right now and not try to give me your opinion or advice. I just need to talk." The fact that you are trying to communicate to your parents is what is most important.

What if you do not have a close and open relationship with your parents? What if you feel there is no way that they could listen to or understand how you are feeling? Even if it looks hopeless, give it a try anyway. They may turn out to be more understanding than you imagined. However, if you try and it flops, then find another adult—teacher, minister, grandparent, aunt, or uncle—to confide in. You might find it easier to talk to one of your friend's parents. One rule to help you decide whom to confide in is to ask yourself, "Does this person really care about me?" If not, find someone else to talk to. There are plenty of adults in your life who do genuinely care about your welfare.

* * *

Teenagers experience greater feelings of trust and security when they can discuss their feelings with their parents. Try to pick a time to talk about your feelings when your parents are not rushed, upset, or tired. It can help to begin by telling your parents that there are some things you would like to talk with them about but that you are also feeling kind of anxious, uncomfortable, or awkward. This will certainly get your parents' attention and will probably make them more sensitive and better listeners. It will also help to tell your parents that you'd like them to listen to everything you have to say before they respond. This can be hard for parents to do, but if you let them know that after you are finished talking, you will be quiet and listen to them, you will probably get their cooperation. Even if you have to bite your tongue, be sure to listen to what they have to say after they have listened to you. Remember, listening to your parents doesn't mean you are agreeing with them or that you have to take their advice.

How do I know if I really need to talk to a psychologist or counselor? *Kristen, age 16*

There are times in everybody's life when talking to a psychologist or counselor is a good idea, like when you feel stuck with a bad feeling or when you don't feel like the answers that you are getting from your usual support systems (your friends, parents, or teachers) are really helping you solve the problem. If you think you need to talk to someone, a good way to make sure you get the most out of it is to make a list of your concerns or problems, or what it is you want to talk about, no matter how silly it sounds. Present your list to the counselor, and ask if those are things they can help you with. Many times they can, and it will only take a few sessions of talking to get you back on track. If you are not sure about whether you need to talk to a psychologist or counselor, try it anyway. It certainly won't hurt.

* * *

There appear to be two main things that bring teens to talk to a psychologist or counselor. One is that they are hurting about something, and it won't go away. Maybe you had an argument with a friend three weeks ago and are still very upset about it. Or maybe your boyfriend suddenly dumped you, and after a month you still feel miserable. A second reason to seek professional help is that you are struggling with things that happened in the past or things you are worried about in the future. For example, maybe your parents got divorced when you were very little, or a grandparent died suddenly. Maybe you can't stop worrying about how you are going to support yourself when it is time to leave home.

When bad feelings persist, or worries just won't go away, it is time to think about speaking to an expert. Talking to a professional will give you some things that talking to your friends or even a trusted adult can't give you. First of all, this professional is neutral so their view of the problem or concern isn't influenced by complicated relationships. Second, your conversations are confidential. And third, the professional is an expert in dealing with problems like yours. So, if you think that you need to talk to somebody confidentially—someone who isn't already involved in your life—then trust your gut feelings and find a professional to help.

Hot Tips

☞ Do you worry about everything you eat? Do you count calories all the time? Do you "binge" eat? These are signs of a possible eating disorder. Get help!

☞ Eating disorders, like anorexia, can be deadly! They are "triggered" by unrealistic fantasies about how a woman should look. Get help if you think you have a problem.

☞ Everyone feels down sometimes. But, if the feeling

lasts for more than a couple of weeks, or is very intense, get help right away. And if you have a friend who is depressed, try to convince her to get help. Depression *can* be treated.

☞ Work on communicating with your parents. Tell them in advance if you are looking for their advice or opinion, or if you just want them to listen.

☞ If you have more than a brief or passing thought about suicide, especially if you're actually putting a plan together, get help immediately.

☞ If you can't stop thinking about something, and it starts to totally control your life, you may have an obsession. There is treatment for obsessions. Talk to your counselor, school nurse, or school psychologist.

☞ Many teens have fears that they are embarrassed or afraid to talk about, but ignoring them won't make them go away. There are ways to overcome your fears.

☞ Anxiety can be a powerful and overwhelming feeling. Slow breathing exercises and relaxation techniques can help. Try them!

☞ Never keep physical or sexual abuse a secret. Get professional help!

☞ Getting help when you need it is a sign of strength and courage, not a weakness.

☞ Don't hesitate to get help for a friend in trouble. Even if your friend gets really angry, it's always better to be safe than sorry.

9

Drugs and Alcohol:
How Can I Not Be Tempted?

Some of my friends use drugs, and some of them drink way too much. I don't want to totally avoid the drinking and drug scene because these kids are my friends. Sometimes I'm so tempted to try stuff. My parents would kill me if they knew any of my friends were doing drugs. They don't even know I smoke! Even though my parents drink too much themselves, they don't think I should drink at all. Drinking and drugs have really messed up a few of my friends, but they just keep on doing it. I wish I could make them stop, but I'd look like such a geek.—*Alison*

Why do I find relief in alcohol? *Bonita, age 19*

Sometimes teens drink alcohol to get relief from stress or to relax. Alcohol is a central nervous system depressant and tends to slow down all of your reactions. That is why it is so dangerous to drive when you have been drinking, even if you've had only one drink. For some teens, alcohol is a way out or an excuse to be out of control. Saying, "I did something I ordinarily would not do, but I was drunk at the time," does not excuse your behavior. And, using alcohol to forget about your problems not only doesn't work but often makes the problem worse. Take a look at what is causing you so much pressure or stress. Then ask yourself, "Is drinking solving my problems, or is it simply covering them up?" Think about how you can work on the problems directly so you can actually do something about it. There is no question that alcohol will give you relief, but it is short-lived and won't really solve anything.

Do you feel that teens grow more if they experiment with drugs and do a little partying, or is it better to be a goody-goody and never try anything? *Liz, age 18*

You are asking a tough and complicated question. It depends on what you mean by "grows" and by "experiment."

Drugs themselves never lead to psychological, emotional, or intellectual growth. So experimenting with a drug will not itself lead to growth. However, learning to manage your life in a culture in which drugs are readily available can lead to all kinds of growth.

Let's back up a minute. Teens learn by experimenting with new kinds of behavior to see how the
behavior fits and feels. Some experiments with new
behavior are potentially dangerous because the consequences or outcomes of the behavior can be physically or emotionally destructive. It is natural to want
to experiment with new forms of awareness, especially
emotional and sensory awareness. So drugs and partying have a special appeal to teens who seek new
experiences. While at the time drug experiences can
be "fun" and "enlightening," there is a huge risk! You
can't tell in advance what will happen if you smoke
a joint, run a couple of lines of coke, drink a few
beers, or drop acid. With all drug use, there is a line
somewhere that separates the experience from being
fun to one that is harmful and dangerous. What
makes experimenting with drugs so dangerous is that
you don't know where the line is until you've crossed
it. You may cross the line the first time you try a drug.
You may cross the line the sixth time you try the drug.
There is just no way of knowing in advance. This
does not mean that you can't go to parties where
there are drugs. It means that you have to decide if
you'll be comfortable at the party if lots of people are
using and you don't.

* * *

Saying no to drugs does not make you a goody-
goody. If you don't want to risk screwing up your life,
you have to learn how to manage in a world full of
all kinds of drugs and quick fixes. You will grow more

from learning how to manage than you ever will from experimenting with drugs. And *now* is not too early to start learning. Even though taking risks is part of being a teenager, it's the *kind* of risks you take that you need to be so careful about. For example, if you don't study for a test and get a really bad grade, it almost never means you will fail the course. Rather, it means that you can't fail too many more tests, or then you will fail the course. But even if you fail the class, you can usually take the class again. So, the risk you took by not studying won't ruin your life.

With drugs though, you can do a lot more damage to yourself and your life than you ever would by failing a test or even a class. It's much, much harder to break a drug or alcohol addiction than it is to make up a test or retake a class. And some of the things that kids do while they are under the influence of drugs or alcohol can *never* be reversed, like seeing a friend overdose and die, having unprotected sex and getting AIDS, or even winding up with a criminal record. If not using drugs or alcohol makes you a "goody-goody," then good for you!

Why do some people think the only way to have fun is with drugs and alcohol?
Roseanne, age 15

People who turn to drugs and alcohol for "fun" probably don't think that it's the *only* way, just the easiest way. They may also be misinformed, particularly about addiction. People who have never been addicted don't know what it means to have drugs or alcohol control their lives. So, they really don't know what they're getting themselves into. They just can't imagine what it is like.

Lots of people (including adults) think that they're an exception, and nothing is going to happen to them. And they come up with excuses for why this is "true." Even though they know how bad addictions can be, they fool themselves into thinking "I'm different. I won't get hooked!" But the truth is you really can't know ahead of time if, or how badly, you are going to get hooked. And if you *do* get hooked, it is very, very difficult to stop. So, experimenting with drugs or alcohol is always a big gamble.

* * *

This is a good question. Alcohol and drugs alter or change the way you behave. You also don't think very well when you are under the influence of drugs or alcohol. When people take drugs or drink too much alcohol, they do things or take risks that they might not if they didn't use drugs or alcohol (like driving a car when they're drunk, riding in a car with a drunk driver, or having sex without really deciding if they want to). Some people think that this is fun or exciting. Another reason why teens use drugs or alcohol is that they are illegal. Some teens think that doing something against the law is fun. While it might seem like fun to drink or do drugs, in the end it often turns out to be no fun at all. Drugs and alcohol can screw up your body and send your school performance downhill. They can mess up your friendships, cause constant fights with your parents, and get you in trouble with the law. There are lots of other ways to have fun, but they require more effort than simply getting high on drugs or alcohol. In the long run, there is no question that the effort pays off.

Why do so many teenagers smoke even though they know it's bad? *Pauline, age 16*

Many people, not just teenagers, do things they know are bad for them. Smoking is bad, but most teenagers have trouble seeing it as bad because the negative effects on your body may not show up for years and years. They tend to overlook that it makes them cough and their breath smell terrible. Most teens (and even adults) kid themselves into thinking that there will always be time to stop before anything really bad happens. The trouble is, cigarettes are addicting so that when you want to stop, it is just not that easy. And even the short-range effects of smoking can be yucky, like longer and more frequent colds.

A lot of teens start to smoke because they think it is "cool." Once they start smoking, it becomes the thing to do when they get together with other kids. It is a shared experience that makes them feel like they belong to a group. Smoking makes some teens feel more grown up. Teens want to be recognized for their maturity and often feel like their parents and other adults still treat them like little children. Smoking is a way some teens try to show that they are not kids anymore. If you want to be treated more like an adult, smoking won't do it. Lighting up won't get adults to treat you differently. Smoking isn't grown up, it's just a slow and nasty way of poisoning yourself.

Why do some people give in to the temptation of drugs and others don't?
June, age 17

People begin using illegal drugs for several reasons. Among the most common are lack of knowledge of the true effects and addictiveness of drugs; rebellion; peer pressure; and a means of escaping from feelings such as boredom, sadness, depression, anxiety, or loneliness. Teens are particularly at risk because of two attitudes and beliefs that many of them hold: one is their tendency to focus on the present and not consider the future, and the other is that most teens feel invulnerable. This means that while they know that drugs can lead to big problems, they fool themselves into believing that nothing bad can happen to them.

There are several things you and your friends can do so you won't be "tempted" to use drugs.

- Find out all you can about drugs, but be careful. Some of the information out there is only aimed to scare you and is not really accurate, whereas other information minimizes the risks. Find out what is really true.

- Make your own honest list of the pros and cons of using drugs. It will help you to see that while drugs may alter your feelings for a short time, they really won't help you change the things in your life that you want to change. Drugs just don't solve problems.

- Don't ignore the *fact* that different drugs are physically and psychologically addictive. This means that the drugs will start controlling you, rather than you controlling them—and you won't see a yellow warning sign—it just happens.

- If you are feeling very tempted to use drugs, remember that you don't need to struggle with this issue alone. Find out where the supports are, whether a school counselor or a drop-in program. And, you can do a lot to help others who are also struggling with this issue!

* * *

At times, it can be really tough to make decisions like whether or not to use drugs. Many teens today feel pressured by the media, their families, and their friends to do things that may or may not feel right to them. What *you* decide about experimenting with drugs may be one of the most critical decisions you are ever faced with. There are many reasons why kids turn to drugs and many reasons why they use drugs. Two of the biggest are how much and how many of their friends use drugs and how close they feel to their parents. Teenagers who use drugs report that they don't feel very close to their parents, they argue with them frequently, and their parents often don't know what they are doing or who they are with. Some of the parents of kids who use drugs have very strict rules at home, and the kids aren't given the opportunity to learn to make decisions for themselves. Others have few or no rules, and while it may look like they "have it easy," they really feel unloved and uncared for.

Basically, adolescents who use hang out with other adolescents who use. Kids who use drugs often feel bad about their schoolwork, may feel lonely or isolated, and often don't receive the support they need at home. They may also have an older brother or sister or parent who drinks or uses drugs, and they may feel that it is normal to start using drugs at an early age. Teenagers who resist the temptation to use drugs are close to their parents and talk to their parents about what is happening in their lives. They have friends who don't use (or use infrequently), and they are invested in their schoolwork, extracurricular activities, and other hobbies and interests.

How do you say no to drugs without looking like a geek? *Dale, age 12*

Tough question! Most important, you have to *want to say no.* If you really want to say yes, you probably will. So the first step is to want to say "no."

The sad truth is that some kids will think you're

a geek if you say no. The good news is that there are other kids who will think you're an idiot if you say yes! You can't have everyone like and accept you, even though you might want to. So, you have to decide which group of kids you want to be part of and then act accordingly.

So how do you say no? In any way that gets the result you want. Some kids fall back on how their parents might punish them: "I'll be grounded for months if my parents ever find out." Or you can say, "Not tonight, I'm just not in the mood." Or, "No thanks, it makes me nauseous." Whatever you say, there are two things to remember: Stick to your "no," and don't judge the other kids who are using. If you judge them, they will judge you. Saying "no" won't make you look like a geek as much as judging your friends will.

Finally, it really helps to stay away from activities where you know there will probably be drugs. It's OK to make up excuses about why you won't be able to attend a certain party or activity. Most of all, remember that sticking to your guns and not being controlled by other kids means you are a strong and independent person.

* * *

It can be really difficult to decide what to do when you are confronted with the opportunity to experiment with drugs. The pressure to use drugs may come from your close friends, older siblings and their friends, or your own feeling that the only way to really fit in is to use drugs. While it may seem like "everyone" uses drugs, in reality, lots of kids don't.

The most important thing to consider in deciding whether or not to say no is to think about how your choice will affect other parts of your life, including your goals for the future. At this time in your life, the choices you make begin to have serious consequences. Using drugs regularly can severely limit your motivation to do things you used to enjoy and excel at, including school, sports, and even social activities. The more you become involved in drug use, the more you are likely to seek out other kids who use drugs regularly. While at first these changes may seem like no big deal, or you may not even notice them, they will eventually make your life more difficult and stressful. Kids who get involved in regular drug use often have strained relationships with their parents and with friends who don't use. Talking to your parents, other adults, or kids who understand how hard it is to say no will definitely help you stay on track. But, in the end, *you* must make the decision for yourself.

* * *

If you want to say no to drugs, then ask yourself, "Why do I think I need to use drugs?" This will lead to other questions about what you want for yourself and whether drugs will really help you or prevent you from achieving your ambitions. The next time someone tries to make you feel like a "geek," keep in mind that being a geek is a lot better than being a victim to the dangers of drug use. If someone offers it to you, simply say "No thanks, I need all my brain cells." It's the kid that's using the drugs who is the real geek!

Do you think that when teenagers act out in ways like getting drunk and smoking that it has to do with their home life?
Erin, age 16

While some kids with difficult home lives act out, so do some with great home lives. Some kids with family problems do just fine, and others don't. A difficult home life is not the only factor in whether or not teens get involved with things like drinking and smoking, but it can be a factor. Some teens drink alcohol, smoke cigarettes, or take drugs to act out or rebel against their parents. Sometimes, parents set a bad example by drinking or smoking themselves. Sometimes teens drink or smoke because their friends do, and they want to fit in or be accepted. Sometimes they want to "experiment." If someone feels unhappy or angry about themselves, school, or their friends, they might drink or smoke to avoid the bad feelings. When people get intoxicated or "high," they often feel a rush of good feelings and a decrease in bad feelings. But, when the rush goes away, the problems are still there. When teens drink or smoke, it's not just for one reason but a combination of reasons.

Whatever the reasons, the outcome is not good. Drinking and smoking are bad for your health and, in the end, don't make problems go away. Actually, they often make things a lot worse and can get you into a lot of trouble. There are always better ways than drinking or smoking to deal with problems. Let someone know that you are having a hard time—a parent, friend, doctor, teacher, school counselor, or someone else you trust. You *can* get help to solve problems in a way that won't be harmful to you.

How do you help a friend address a drinking or drug problem? *Connie, age 17*

Adolescents rarely want to admit that they might have a problem with drinking or drugs. In fact, most adolescents who end up in substance abuse treatment only get there because of pressure from parents or the legal system. The best way to approach your friend is by being open and nonjudgmental. Share your own feelings and experiences about how you have been afraid to deal with some of your own problems and issues. This is the best way to encourage your friend to be honest about his or her own worries. For example, tell your friend about how her drinking and drug use has changed the way she behaves and why you are so concerned. Often, you can have greater influence on your friends' decisions and choices than any adults.

People who use heavily may withdraw, act depressed or irritable, or start to talk about hurting themselves. These are all very serious signs of drug abuse or dependence. If you have a strong friendship and believe that your friend's alcohol or drug problem is severe enough that it is threatening her health or safety, talk to a trusted adult. Even if your friend gets really mad at you, it is definitely better than having her seriously hurt herself. Trust your judgment and get help if you are really afraid for your friend. Once your friend is in recovery, she'll be grateful.

* * *

Do you remember a time in your life when someone told you that something you were doing was a problem? For example, maybe one of your parents lectured you about smoking. Or a teacher told you that you weren't working up to your potential. Didn't you feel criticized? Defensive? And maybe even angry? Whenever anyone "confronts" us, especially if there is some truth in what they are saying, we tend to push them away or defend ourselves. You can expect the same reaction from your friend when you confront her about her drinking or drug use. So, don't expect thanks for your intervention. But, do it anyway. It is your responsibility as a friend to try to get her to see that she has a problem.

However, this is where your responsibility ends. You cannot make your friend stop. Stopping is her decision, and it is not your fault if she ignores your caring advice.

When speaking of family alcoholism, is it really true that you will become an alcoholic if your father and grandfather are? *Faith, age 17*

If your father or grandfather is an alcoholic, this does *not* mean for sure that you will have this problem. There are a lot of other things, besides having a family member who is an alcoholic, that influence whether a person develops a problem with alcohol. For example, teens who hang out with friends who drink alcohol are more likely to drink. Also, teens who try to cover up their problems instead of talking about them might be more likely to drink. There isn't *one* thing that will make you an alcoholic. It's usually a combination of reasons.

But there are things that you can do to avoid this problem. The first is to recognize that alcoholism is a problem; then you can choose to associate with people who don't drink or do drugs. If you start to have problems, like with school, family members, or friends, talk to someone you trust and get help. Don't turn to drugs or alcohol. Having a family member who is an alcoholic can put you at greater risk, but it definitely does not mean you are going to become an alcoholic. Like so many other things you are faced with, it's what *you* decide to do that makes the difference.

* * *

Some people are born predisposed to a higher risk of becoming addicted to alcohol. This means that they may have "inherited" the vulnerability to become alcoholics from their parents or grandparents. For these people, it is much harder to stop drinking once they start. And when they do drink, they may have a really bad reaction. They may get very sick and black out, or they may become depressed, violent, or reckless. While nobody turns to alcohol because they want these reactions, these things can happen. If there is a history of drinking in your family, you need to be very careful. Alcohol is a sedative, and some people find that drinking it relieves the pressure and stress they are feeling or reduces their bad feelings. A glass of wine or other drink on occasion is not harmful, but excessive and continual drinking can significantly alter your ability to think clearly and be in control of your own behavior. If alcoholism runs in your family, assume that you are more likely to become an alcoholic than any of your friends who don't have this history.

How are you supposed to live with someone who is drinking and you are uncomfortable with it? *Rachel, age 12*

It's really hard living with someone who drinks too much. It's hard in lots of ways. You never know how the person's going to act. You don't know if it's safe to bring friends into your own home. You might even try to change your behavior hoping it will help. (It never really does.) Have you tried talking with one of your parents? If it's one of your parents who is drinking, the other parent needs to know it bothers you. Sometimes parents don't want to face the fact that someone they love has a drinking problem. Two true things to remember during the bad days are that you can't stop the person from drinking, and it isn't your fault. There's a group called Alanon for Teens (Ala-Teen). Many kids find that it helps to talk with other kids about how it feels to have a family member who drinks.

* * *

First, trust your feelings! If you are uncomfortable with the person's drinking, you have good reason to feel uncomfortable. Second, remember that you probably won't be able to solve this problem on your own because someone with a drinking problem usually creates a lot of difficulties in the family. One of the biggest is that most problem drinkers insist they don't have a problem, and they get really angry with anyone who suggests they do. Problem drinkers really need to protect their drinking lifestyle, which makes it incredibly hard for them to accept that they might need help.

So, even though it is a good idea to try to talk with a problem drinker, don't be surprised or discouraged if you can't get her or him to listen. Instead, find a responsible adult *you* can talk to about what is going on and how you feel. Often, a school counselor, minister, rabbi, or priest can be very helpful. Or there might be an older person in your family—a brother, sister, aunt, grandparent, or parent—you can talk to. In deciding who to talk to, you need to be as sure as you can that this person will keep your confidence.

There's also lots of help available in most communities. Ala-Teen (check the local phone book for the one near you) can be a really good place to contact. Ala-Teen holds meetings for teens who have a problem drinker in their family. When you call, the adult you speak with can tell you what kind of help is available, including other resources in your community. Help is available, so don't try to go it alone.

All of these sources of help will tell you one very important thing: You are not the *cause* of this person's drinking, you are not responsible for what this person does when she or he drinks, and you need to protect yourself from the negative consequences of this person's drinking. The bottom line is it's not your fault, and you can't stop her or him. But, you can get help for yourself.

* * *

For kids and adolescents growing up in alcoholic homes, one of the most important things is to have someone they trust whom they can talk to about their fears and concerns. One of the worst things you can do is to keep everything inside and take responsibility for the person who is drinking too much, particularly if it is a parent. Kids from alcoholic homes often believe that they should and can make their parent stop drinking. Sometimes they try to get better grades, do more chores, excel more in sports, or have fewer friends and spend more time at home. These things won't work.

Teenage girls who are children of alcoholics often find themselves faced with the burden of taking care of an alcoholic parent and feeling responsible for this parent's problems. They often feel ashamed to talk to their friends or even other relatives about what is happening, and they wind up feeling completely alone. One of the best things you can do for yourself is to find friends who are going through similar experiences. Many schools and community organizations have counseling groups for teens from alcoholic homes. Listening to other kids talk about their feelings can help ease the intensity of your own fears and frustrations. In addition, talking to another adult about your worries can help to ease the shame of having a parent who drinks too much.

Hot Tips

☞ You *can* say no to drugs and alcohol if you really want to.

☞ If someone in your house drinks too much, remember that it's not your fault. And, you can get help to cope with the situation. Check out groups such as Ala-Teen. Don't try to "go it alone."

☞ Using drugs, alcohol, or cigarettes might seem cool or make you feel grown up, but addictions are no fun at all—and they can really mess up your life, permanently.

☞ There are positive ways of dealing with troubles at home. Escaping through drugs and alcohol won't help.

☞ Although alcoholism does tend to run in families, this does not mean that you're doomed. But it does mean that you have to be especially careful.

☞ If a friend is in big trouble with drugs or alcohol and won't listen to you, get help. Even if your friend gets really mad, you won't regret it.

☞ While alcohol does relieve stress temporarily, after a while it can make you feel more depressed. And, it doesn't do a thing to solve your problems.

☞ Not doing drugs does not make you a "goody-goody." It means you are a really strong and wise young woman.

☞ Some of the choices you make today can seriously impact your life tomorrow. While it's normal to make mistakes, you already know the dangers of drugs, alcohol, and smoking, so there's no excuse.

10

What Will My Future Be Like?

I think a lot about my future. What will I be like? What will I do? I have lots of dreams about what I'll be like when I grow up, but I don't know how I'll ever make all those decisions. Adults have so many responsibilities, I can't imagine how I'll be able to do it all. Sometimes it feels kind of scary. It would be so much easier to just stay being a kid.—*Jenny*

Why is the future so scary? *Ida, age 16*

Even if it seems a bit boring at times, we all feel more comfortable with the known than with the unknown. And, what we know about is the past and the present. The future is always an unknown. Change can seem too big to imagine and too hard to handle. And, as a teen, you're already going through a lot of changes: your feelings change frequently; your body is changing its shape and size; and your friendships, family connections, and school situation may also be changing. With things so unpredictable inside and outside of you, it may often seem as if it would be much safer if you could know what the future holds in store for you.

Since none of us can know exactly what our future will be like, here are three things you can do so the future won't feel quite so scary to you: (1) Pay attention to the things you have some control over; make plans about the parts of your life that you feel you can predict or anticipate; (2) gather information about whatever it is you wish you knew more about; and (3) try thinking differently about the scary picture in your head. For instance, do you want to go to college? This part of your future is largely up to you, and there's lots that you can do about it now. You can get college catalogues; you can think about whether you want to be in a city or rural setting; you can visit some colleges. You can study hard, so that your grades help you get into the college you want, and so on. And, if the idea of going away to college feels only scary to you, stop and make a list of the things you can do in college that you really, really want, like having no curfew, or being able to choose classes you want to take. It's like changing the frame on a picture. One frame doesn't look very good, and the other makes the picture look terrific. Instead of describing the future as "scary," you might try words like "exciting" or "an adventure." This can help you balance your scared feelings with eagerness.

* * *

Sometimes the future feels scary for all of us because we can't control everything that will happen in the future. You may ask yourself, "Will I be able to do all the things I want to as I get older? Will I find someone to love and be loved by? Will I be successful in whatever I choose to do with my life? And, even if all these things work out well, what will happen if the world pollutes itself out of existence, or wars end life as we now know it?" The bottom line is that in a world with so many uncertainties, we can only do the best we can. We can make plans for our lives and work to achieve our goals and our dreams. Throughout history, people have had many of the same fears. While no one of us can control the world or solve all of the world's problems, we can take control of our own lives and do what we can to make the future seem less scary. For some people, the belief in a higher power gives them comfort and support in thinking about the future. So, try to avoid using up too much of your energy worrying ahead of time about what *might* happen, and use it toward the things you can control. Remember, the famous writer Mark Twain said, "I worried about living a terrible life, most of which never happened."

Am I normal in my feelings of uncertainty and fear about the future? *Iris, age 18*

You are very normal. In fact, most kids your age don't know what they want to do in the future and this can be rather frightening. You may have a friend who's got her future all plotted out and wonder what's wrong with you. Well cool for her, but she's not the norm; most kids don't know exactly what they want to do, even by the end of high school. But, this is a good time to start focusing on some ideas. You might start a journal. Give it a fun title and write about the things you think about for your future—include your fears, your wishes, and your dreams. If you read about something that you might like to try, clip it out and put it in your "future" journal. Or, if you see something on TV or in the movies that you like, add it. For now, don't limit yourself. Put your dreams right beside your fears. Both are equally important in helping you to sort out your future.

* * *

Yes! You are totally normal. There is far too much pressure on teenagers today to decide what they want to do when they grow up. It is perfectly normal, and in fact most teenagers do not decide on a career at this time in their lives. This is the time in your life for exploration. How can you possibly decide what you want for your future when you have only been on the planet for such a short time? It is hard to know what you want if you haven't had the opportunity to experience it. How would you know if you wanted to be an astronaut unless you knew what astronauts do? And another thing to remember: Research suggests that these days many people go through several careers in a lifetime. So, the career you pick as a young adult may not be the one you stick with your whole life. Now is not the time to find *the* answer, it's the time to ask lots of questions.

Will I achieve my dreams? *Rosie, age 12*

That's a hard question to answer because while we can do many things to work toward achieving our dreams, we cannot control everything. In spite of this, it is very important not to let go of your dreams and to get support and guidance from those around you. It takes a lot of work to reach most dreams. If you are not sure that your dreams fit with your skills or talents, don't hesitate to ask people who know you well. You might ask them, "Can you imagine me being a teacher, a sports writer, or an accountant?" One of the best ways to explore your dreams is by starting now to read and talk with people who seem to be doing the kind of work or living the kind of life you'd like to have. Don't be afraid to ask them how they got where they are. Most people will feel flattered and be willing to share some or all of the steps they took to get where they now are. So, hold on to your dreams, but don't think they will come true without your help and your hard work.

* * *

Dreams about what our future will hold are very important. They represent our hopes and ideas about what we want our future to be like. Our dreams give us something to work toward, something to live for. Our dreams constantly change as we grow and as our life changes. When you were little, and someone asked you what you wanted to be when you grew up, you might have said a princess or a ballerina. Today, your dreams for the future are probably quite different. For example, right now you might dream of being an artist, living in a large city, working in a studio loft with other artists. And you may wind up doing just that! However, as you learn about art and study its history, and as you meet other artists, you could wind up being an art teacher, or running a gallery, or even being a cartoonist. The idea is to enjoy exploring your dreams. Also make room for new dreams and visions, and don't be afraid to let your dreams change. Exploring your dreams is as important as achieving them.

How do I decide my future? How do I make it happen? *Beth, age 13*

Look in the mirror and ask yourself, "What do I really enjoy doing? What makes me feel happy, productive, and proud of myself?" It might be sports, music, math, quilting, helping others, working with kids, or a million other things. You might even make a list of all the things you think of, and keep working on it, maybe for a week or a month. Then, take your list and pick two or three things you'd like to focus on. Begin thinking about whether any of the things you are now doing are helping you to explore your interests. Are you on a sports team? Are you in the school band? Are you doing some volunteer work with kids or the elderly? Don't think yet about specific jobs or careers. Stay focused on the things you feel passionate about. This is the time of your life to explore possibilities, not to limit yourself.

* * *

First, don't get too stressed out about deciding what to do with your life right now. In the end, most adults are pretty happy with their lives, and very few say they wish they were someone else. And, if you start off in one direction, and are not happy with it, it's more than OK to decide to take another path. There are stories about great mathematicians who decided to become cooks, and architects who decided to become ski instructors, and secretaries who went on to become great trial lawyers. In today's world, there are lots of opportunities to change careers midstream. While your choice of career is certainly important, it alone won't make you happy. Learning how to get along with others, finding meaningful relationships with girls and guys, and learning to like who you are will all prepare you for a happy and successful life. So ... it's a two part deal. Exploring your interests and exploring relationships are both really important.

Why am I afraid of becoming an adult and taking on adult responsibilities?
Fatma, age 14

You are not alone. Lots of teens today have fears and anxieties about entering the adult world. For most people, change is very exciting and very nerve-wracking at the same time! You probably hear adults, like your parents, friends' parents, or relatives, talk about their lives and the problems and concerns they have. Listening to all of this might make you feel overwhelmed. At this time in your life, imagining yourself with all the responsibilities of adulthood can seem like a place you'd never want to get to. You might worry about how hard it would be to leave your family, friends, school, and community. And, while the idea that your parents still have some control over you might irritate and annoy you, the idea of having so much responsibility and having to make all your decisions on your own could feel like a bit much. Fortunately, the path to adulthood is a slow one, it doesn't happen overnight. So be assured that if you slowly and surely work on becoming more independent and more responsible for yourself, when the time comes, you will feel ready to enter the adult world.

How do I evolve from confusion and chaos to a capable, strong, compassionate woman? *Ellen, age 15*

You'll need time and life experience, and the fact that you are already asking such a thoughtful and mature question suggests that you are probably already well on your way. People who reflect on these things are often the ones who need to worry about them the least. Trust yourself as you make choices in your life. Try to keep your choices in line with your values and beliefs. Make up your own mind; don't let others tell you how to think or how you should feel. Being honest with yourself about your strengths and weaknesses, treating others the way you would like to be treated, having the strength to stand up for your values and beliefs, and most importantly, believing in yourself, are the most important things you can do to become the woman you want to be.

* * *

One of the most important things you need to do to become the person you want to be is to spend some time in your own company, doing things that help you think about and discover who you are. Reading, writing in a journal, and taking the time to think about the things you have done each day and the way you have interacted with others will help you get a handle on who you are as a person. For example, if you want to become a compassionate woman, then think about the ways in which you listen to other people, support them in their struggles, and express joy for their successes. Exploring your strengths means getting out into the world and finding out what you are good at and what you enjoy, and then taking the time to think about what part of these experiences made you feel good. It is always helpful to talk with older teens and adult women who you admire and find out what makes them capable, strong, and compassionate.

If you don't know what you want from life, how are you supposed to make important decisions about your future?
Dana, age 17

The first thing to remember is that very few decisions are written in stone. Especially the ones that teenagers normally face. While there are certainly decisions that could change the course of your life forever, or even end it, most of the decisions you need to make at this point in your life are not irreversible. You could pick a college, and then transfer if you weren't happy; you could learn to play an instrument, and then stop or switch; you could study Latin, and then never again take another Latin course. Each of these decisions is an opportunity to learn more about what you *do* and *don't* want in your future. Even though some decisions may seem really hard to make, there are a few things that can be helpful to remember.

1. Most of the decisions you make now are not permanent. Try seeing them as experiences that lead you to knowing more about yourself and what you want.
2. Look at the decisions you make in your life right now as giving you the opportunity to try out things that will help you make other decisions later on.
3. Remember that if you are careful to avoid making decisions that are reckless or self-destructive, all you risk losing is some time.
4. And most importantly, don't make a habit of avoiding making decisions because you don't know what you want from life. *Not* deciding anything won't help you find your way.

Does rebellion during the teenage years lead to any long-term effects on a person such as in her job and her receptiveness to authority? *Sara, age 18*

It depends! Some rebellious behaviors, such as occasionally skipping a class, missing a few curfews, or briefly experimenting with drinking, are likely to have few, if any, long-term effects. More serious rebellious behaviors (like truancy from school, running away from home, promiscuous sex, or excessive drinking or drug use) can potentially have major long-term consequences, from becoming a parent before you want to, to catching serious diseases, to legal problems. These kinds of consequences will surely affect your life and, while some can be changed or altered with a lot of hard work, think about whether or not you really want to create these kinds of problems for yourself.

* * *

The answer to this question depends on the kind of rebellious behaviors you engage in, your motivation to rebel, and what you learn from your experiences. Normal "rebellion," or rebellion that is unlikely to have long-term consequences, is healthy. It is the way teens question authority and begin to think for themselves, which is an important step on the road to becoming a thoughtful adult. On the one hand, some younger teens (age 12–13) question almost everything their parents or other authority figures say, and by the time they are age 16 or 17, they don't feel that their parents "know" much that is of value to them. On the other hand, some teens tell their parents a great deal and then argue about every decision they make. Both paths can lead to becoming a successful adult and parent. The truth is that as you get older, your parents will continue to have less and less control over you, and you can say and do more and more of what you want. There's a hitch here, though. You've got to be willing to accept the consequences. The bottom line is that your "rebellion" belongs to you, and only you can choose to learn from your experience and decide what behaviors will and will not cause you potential big trouble.

How are we influenced by the media?
Taryn, age 18

The media has a huge impact on all of our lives in many ways. To begin with, the news we get each day influences us simply because the particular newspapers, magazines, or TV stations choose what to present to us and what to leave out. If you only listen to or read one news report (like the TV news instead of a newspaper or the Internet), then you may not get a complete picture of a story because of how that particular media source chose to present it. Therefore, in order to get a balanced view and different opinions, you need to read or listen to more than one media report.

As entertainment or advertising, the media can strongly influence our opinions and decisions about almost everything, from what we wear, to what we eat, to how we spend our spare time. The commercial media wants to influence us because they are trying to sell their product or point of view. Your job is to not be an easy sale. Your job is to resist believing that a particular product or point of view is the best one or the right one just because the media says so. Learning to treat the media with caution will go a long way in helping you to be sure that how you spend your time and money is right for you.

What do dreams mean? *Janet, age 11*

What a great question! Sometimes we wake up in the morning after having very strange dreams that don't make sense to us. Many people think that dreams are about things that you're not exactly aware of but are on your mind. It's sort of like when you have a fight with a friend and then later that day you snap at your brother and don't know why. Your fight with your friend was really bothering you, even though you weren't exactly thinking about it the moment you yelled at your brother. The fight was on your mind, but you weren't really aware of it. Dreams are kind of the same way. They can be about things that you are worried about or problems that you might have. Dreams can also be about wishes or things that you want to happen. While sometimes you can understand what a dream means, many times they are pretty complicated and hard to figure out.

* * *

For many years, there has been a great deal of debate about the meaning of dreams. Some say dreams mean nothing, but a number of famous psychiatrists, such as Sigmund Freud, believed that dreams definitely have meaning. Some experts believe that dreams are a way of delivering a message from the dreamer's unconscious mind to his or her conscious mind. For example, the egg is supposed to be a universal symbol for birth or rebirth. Therefore, some experts believe that if you dream about an egg it might mean that an aspect of your personality that is hidden (not yet born) is trying to come out (and be born again). Freud believed that dreams are either a person's attempt to work out conflicts that are un-resolved during the day or a way to fulfill a wish. Very often, the real meaning of dreams is hard for us to understand because in our dreams, our minds use sym-bolism rather than concrete, clear images (like an egg representing the desire to become more outgoing). Some experts believe that the real meaning of our dreams is "hidden" because our dreams often contain difficult thoughts that our conscious minds want to avoid.

Dreams about conflicts we have not been able to resolve, or wishes we have not been able to fulfill during the day, are about pretty intense stuff. For ex-ample, here is one adolescent girl's dream: "I'm a young child and my mom is giving me a birthday party in the garage of our house. In the garage, there are many black widow spiders. In my dream, I can see the spiders hanging from the ceiling on their webs. My mother doesn't notice the spiders and goes on with the birthday party as if nothing is wrong." In real life, this girl's mother has allowed her to date older guys since she was only 12. One interpretation of this dream is that the girl's mother needed to relive her own adolescence by allowing her daughter to date older guys who were "hunks." The black widow spi-ders in the dream represent danger. The girl's mother refuses to see the danger of the spiders and just goes on with the party, not seeing her daughter's fears. The conflict that the girl could not resolve was that she wanted to please her mom, but she could not handle the pressures for sex that the older guys were putting on her. Her dream represents her conflict between her own need to be protected and her need to please her mother. For each of us, it is our unique mind that produces our dreams. We will probably never know for sure if any of our dream interpretations are correct, but dreams sure can be fun to try to analyze.

Hot Tips

☞ Hold on to your dreams for the future, and do everything you can to make them come true.

☞ Learn as much as you can about different careers, but don't pressure yourself to make a decision now. It's too early.

☞ This is the time for exploration. Try new things and explore new interests.

☞ Becoming an adult can seem overwhelming at times. Remember that it doesn't happen over-night—you'll get there one step at a time.

☞ You can learn many things from books, but some things can only be learned through life experi-ences. Becoming a strong and capable woman takes time.

☞ If the future seems scary to you, you're not alone. Many teens feel this way. Talk to your friends—you'll feel better.

☞ Most decisions you make now are not written in stone. You're supposed to make mistakes—the idea is to learn from them.

☞ One of the best ways to explore different careers is to talk to someone in the field, or ask if you can follow them for a day. You'll learn a lot, and they'll be flattered that you asked.

☞ The media is often out to "sell" a product or opinion; they don't always tell the "whole truth." Check out different sources before you totally believe something you see or read.

☞ Your dreams can give you important cues about your wishes, fears, and conflicts. Take a closer look and see if you can figure them out.

11

Why Is It So Hard to "Fit In"?

There are so many groups and cliques in my school. I want to fit in, but I don't want to change myself just so others will accept me. But if you're not part of a group, it's like you have no life, and other kids make fun of you. The peer pressure is so strong. Some kids are really critical and prejudiced. Why are we judged so much by how we look, how rich we are, or our skin color?—*Sylvana*

Why do I care so much about my appearance and what people think of my clothes, hair, and so on? *Olivia, age 16*

Your physical appearance sends important messages to others about how you think and feel about yourself. The way you wear your hair, make-up, and clothing is one way of letting others know about your taste, style, and the groups you identify with (like the jocks, the preps, the "druggies"). People do make judgments about you based on your appearance and assume things about you from the way you look. Let's try a few examples. What judgments would you make about the following girls?

- Sara wears all black all the time. Her face is whitened with face paint and her lipstick is very dark black. Her clothes are often wrinkled and sometimes they are dirty. Her hair is long and straight and often looks oily. She has a butterfly tattoo on her ankle.
- Jessie is tall and thin and her hair is cut very short. She never wears make-up or earrings. She almost always wears either baggy jeans with a white T-shirt or overalls and a white T-shirt. Sometimes she is mistaken for a boy.
- DeeDee wears a variety of clothes, but all of them are in style—pants, jeans, short dresses, long skirts, and a variety of colors, but she likes purple best. Her hair is long and it always looks very full-bodied and clean. She wears eyeliner, and she often has a couple of butterfly barrettes in her hair.

Think about the labels and assumptions you were making about these girls as you were reading the descriptions of their appearance. It's likely that your assumptions aren't all true, but it's a good bet that at least half of them are right on target. So, whether we like it or not, appearance is one of the ways you communicate about who you are.

* * *

This is the time in your life when you are working to explore your identity and how you are going to express yourself as a person. How you dress, use or don't use make-up, style your hair, and so on are ways of expressing yourself. The teen years are a time for experimenting with different ways of communicating who you are. So, it is not unusual for teens to change their appearance during this time. Don't be surprised if one day you wake up and find that you no longer like the clothes you've been wearing or your hair style. Suddenly, these things don't seem to "fit" you any more. This simply means that your changing self wants to express itself in new ways. It is natural for you to want to change the way you look to reflect your emerging self. For most teens, "appearance" is a very important way of communicating with their peers, so it is also natural that you are concerned about what others think about your looks.

Why do we criticize someone who has different tastes, styles, or feelings than the majority? *Lisette, age 17*

The way we value and judge anything around us is usually based on what we are familiar with, or what is often called the "norm." Often, when we see something different, we raise our eyebrows, and say

"What's that?" in a judgmental way. In short, people tend to criticize things, people, tastes, and styles that are different from the norm. For example, after traveling to a far corner of the world, one girl was describing to her class that on her trip she had eaten snake. As soon as her classmates heard that she had eaten something they could never imagine eating, the entire class began laughing hysterically. Even when the girl tried to tell the class that snake tastes just like chicken, they kept laughing. Clearly, the very idea of eating snake was so strange that others could only laugh at her. When others criticize you, you have to make a very important decision. Do you let it go or do you stand up for yourself? Only you can decide whether or not to speak up, but in making this decision, it's important to be sure that you are not keeping quiet because you are afraid but because the issue just isn't that important to you. When something is important, stand up for yourself and work hard to get others to listen to your opinions and feelings. Try telling them why you think or feel the way you do, and suggest to them that while you are not trying to change their thoughts or beliefs, it won't hurt them to listen to yours. While this won't work all the time, you will help some people to become more open and appreciative of different tastes, styles, and feelings.

* * *

For some people, tastes, styles, and opinions that are different from theirs make them uncomfortable. They feel anxious and defensive, and they often don't even listen before they start criticizing. When we don't understand how someone could possibly like something we don't, we stereotype them in a way that puts down their position in order to make ourselves feel one-up and more powerful. This is one of the ways that some people try to maintain their sense of security. If you find that you tend to behave like this when you are confronted with things or ideas that don't reflect your taste, style, or feelings, try to at least keep from criticizing others. Criticizing others simply because they have different likes than you only makes you appear close-minded.

Why do we judge people based on their looks? *Emma, age 15*

Looks are the first thing we have to react to when we meet someone. As human beings, looks are one of the things we use to decide whether another person is "safe" or "dangerous." The problem is that while looks can tell us a little about a person, many people use someone's appearance alone to decide whether or not that person is "likable" or worthy of being their friend. From your question, it is clear that you are already aware that looks are a superficial and ineffective way to judge anyone. And, people who judge others solely on their appearance are often afraid to get to know a person who looks different from themselves, their family, or their friends. Sometimes, it takes real courage to work toward getting to know people who look different and who we are not comfortable with at first sight. But, if you let looks be the deciding factor, you'll lose out because you will never find out who that person really is. So while looks can give you some clues, they don't give you the answer.

* * *

When we do not know someone, we use all of the easily available tools to decide what they are like and what we might expect from them. Many people use a person's looks as one of those tools and make inaccurate assumptions about what a person is like underneath. The problem is that more than half the time, they are wrong! We actually learn very little about a person from how they look. However, because it is easy and fast, we are likely to do it even when we try not to.

How can I get people to stop looking at me as not part of their group and as not important? *Antoinette, age 13*

Unfortunately, there are always going to be people who make judgments about you on the basis of how you look—the color of your skin, your hair style, your weight, your clothes, where you live, and how much money your family seems to have. Being seen as "not as good" or "unimportant" is something that people, particularly those whose skin color happens not to be white, have had to deal with all their lives. What is important for you to remember is that while you may not be able to control how other people act or react to you, you can control how *you* react. So, look at people who judge you as unimportant as the ones with the problem. Focus on surrounding yourself with people who build your sense of self (family and friends) and always regard yourself as important. What you think of yourself is what really matters!

* * *

One of the ways to get "in" with a group you want to be accepted by is for you to start talking to the people you wish would start talking to you. It takes a lot of courage, but if you just sit back and wait, you can almost be guaranteed that nothing will change. So, get up your courage and start a conversation with someone in the group. Try saying something neutral and pleasant to begin with, such as "I really like your shirt" or "I saw you make that soccer goal," or maybe you can even make a comment about a class you are in together. It may not work all the time, but it will work sometimes. Choosing to speak up tells other people that you believe that you are important and can help to get others to treat you that way.

How can I not change myself just to fit in?
ToniMae, age 15

Many teens struggle with this very question. We all want to fit in. Fitting in makes us feel worthy and acceptable, and who doesn't want that? Sometimes, it can be really hard to fit in, but here are some things to remember that might help.

First, remind yourself that you are *always* changing. We change how we feel, what we like, and what we want to do all the time. Second, during your teen years, you are supposed to try on new and different ways of thinking and acting until you find the ones that fit for you. In order to find out what fits for you and where you fit in, you have to try out many different ways of acting and being. If you try something that does not work for you, you are always free to change it, no matter what your friends say. Teens who "change" only to "fit in" often become increasingly uncomfortable because they aren't being themselves. It's like trying to walk in a pair of shoes that are too small. During adolescence, it is normal to be confused and to not be sure of who you are. You might try this. Once a month, do a private "check-in" with yourself. Ask yourself, "Do I like who I've been during the past month? Have I been trying so hard to fit in that I've lost parts of myself that I like?" Remember not to be too hard on yourself. You are simply exploring who you are. As you move toward adulthood, you *will* find your way.

* * *

No one should feel obligated to change themselves in order to fit into a group. But, some kids want to fit in so badly that they pay a very high price: They try to change who they are, which never works for long. If you don't fit into a certain group, think twice before trying to mold yourself into someone that you are not. Consider the possibility that the group may not be right for you. Some groups don't accept things and people who are different than themselves, like people of different ages, races, religions, or sexual orientation. Other groups may keep you out because you are not into the same things they are: sports, music, or maybe even drugs. One of the best ways to "hold onto yourself" and not try to change yourself just to fit in is to work on trusting and believing that *your* thoughts and feelings are as valid as anyone else's. At the same time, take the time to listen to and experience the differences between you and other people. Even when you don't agree, you can still let others know that you appreciate the differences. Experiencing differences, including your own, is one of the greatest gifts we can give ourselves. So don't miss out.

Why is society so unfair toward women?
Lucinda, age 14

The way society treats women is a problem with a long history and has a lot to do with power. For centuries, in the vast majority of the world, men have been the "boss." For example, this might surprise you: In England, even though for centuries there have been queens, women were not allowed to own property. In the United States, when most of your grandmothers were born, women had not yet been given the right to vote. You might want to read about the

Women's Suffrage Movement in the United States to learn the story about how hard women had to fight just to be able to vote. In our society today, women constantly get double messages: "Be smart, but not too smart, or the guys won't like you." "Be pretty, but don't act slutty, because it's OK for guys to like sex but not for girls." "Be strong, but don't show it, because girls aren't supposed to be as strong as boys." Don't believe any of these double messages. They are wrong! The first step in changing how society treats women is to do just what you are doing—notice that women *are* treated differently than men and speak up. Tell others, "It is not OK to treat me (or other women) unfairly." For example, expect to get the same pay as a guy for doing the same job. If you want to play a sport for which your school only has a boys' team, speak up. Girls are equal to boys and are entitled to equal treatment!

* * *

In most societies, including ours, men dominate in their families, in their workplace, in civic organizations, government, and organized religions. Women are often given less favorable tasks, less powerful roles, or roles and tasks that are less valued than the roles and tasks that men are given. In a household, women are often expected to do the chores, and at work they are often paid less than men and are given lower positions. While society has changed a great deal, and women's roles today have expanded beyond being the home maker, unfortunately, many people (both men

214

and women) still expect women to keep their home-making responsibilities at the same time that they hold full-time jobs. So, women are often expected to have a double career: one at work, and another at home. If women are going to achieve total equality with men, we as a society and you as an individual must continue to expect and work toward equality for women. You can start right now by making sure you value the brains and talents you have, as well as those of the women around you. While you may think you value women equally to men, give yourself this quick test and try to answer these questions really honestly:

- "Do I secretly think men are really smarter than women?"
- "If I like a guy, do I hide my brains and talent just a little?"

If your answer to either of these questions is "yes," you've probably been taught to see women as less than men. So, watch yourself and pay attention to your own unequal thinking. Sometimes, we don't even realize that we are thinking and behaving in ways that value men more than women.

Why do people make fun of others?
Katrina, age 13

The simple answer is that people make fun of others to make themselves feel better. People who need to "put others down" by making hurtful remarks are really very insecure—and they try to feel important by making others feel unimportant. Underneath, they don't believe that they themselves are very worthwhile. Often, these people focus their hurtful remarks or behaviors on someone who is different, someone they think will be easy to pick on, who can't easily defend her or himself. These people try to be popular at the expense of others, but they are really very unfortunate because they are ruled by fear and low self-esteem.

* * *

Sometimes people make fun of others simply because they are uncomfortable with people who are different from them and they are ignorant or insecure about who they are. Sometimes, these people simply have nothing else to do, so they pick on others. When someone makes fun of you, one of the best things you can do is to ignore them and walk away immediately. When you turn away, you deprive the person of any of the "enjoyment" they might get from teasing or hurting you. But, if someone is *really* bullying and harassing you, you may need to tell someone like your school counselor, a teacher, or your parents so they can help you to deal with the situation and hold the bully accountable for his or her unacceptable behavior.

Why are things so divided by wealth? What is the best way to overcome this barrier? *Margaret, age 13*

You've asked a really good question. The forces that divide our society by wealth are very complicated, and so are the solutions. The best way to deal with an issue like this (one you have little or no control over) is to make a real effort not to act or think in ways that contribute to the very problem you wish would go away. This means don't judge people by how much money they have or don't have, and don't assume just because someone's family seems to have a lot of money that they are "richer" than you are. While money can buy many things, it cannot buy happiness. Most importantly, don't judge your own worth by how much money you or your family has. It's often hard when people around you put value on material things rather than on inner wealth (a person's character). Remember that "riches" are not really counted in dollar bills.

* * *

Wealth is easy to see, to count, and to touch. People can easily see what brand of tennis shoes you wear, what kind of house or neighborhood you live in, what kind of car you or your parents drive, where you shop, and where you go on vacation. While wealth should not serve to separate or divide people, it often does. And sadly, some people use wealth as the basis for deciding on who they will socialize with and who will be their friends. The people who do this often have no idea how much they are missing by making their world so small. One of the best ways to overcome the barrier of wealth is to be open to meeting people from different economic groups. You can do this by looking for and joining in activities that are open to a diverse group of people from different social, racial, ethnic, and economic groups. Many such activities probably exist in your school, community center, or church, like picnics, camping trips, or visits to the mountains. Volunteer opportunities can also bring together a diverse group of people. When you have the experience of sharing a common activity, differences such as how much money people have often melt away.

Why is it so tempting to give in to peer pressure? *Teresa, age 17*

It is very tempting to give in to peer pressure because, at the time, it seems to be so much safer and easier to give in and belong than to risk rejection and be labeled an outsider. As you grow older and mature, the temptation to give in to peer pressure and the ability to stand alone when something is important to you increases. You find more and different ways to satisfy your needs for acceptance and positive self-esteem. For now, it might help to try making a list of the pros and cons of giving in to the things you feel pressured about. For example, let's say that at some parties, some of your friends sneak outside to have a beer. And let's say that even though you don't feel that having a beer is such a big deal, you really don't want to get involved with the drinking because you don't think it's worth the trouble you'd get into if you got caught. So now you have what we call an "approach-avoidance" conflict. You want to fit in, which means going out for that beer, and at the same time, you don't want trouble, which means staying in and not drinking. Take a look at the benefits you'll get from going out, and compare them with the benefits you'll get from staying in. While you might feel cool being out with the drinkers, you'll probably also feel pretty nervous and be watching over your shoulder because you are afraid of getting caught. And, even if you don't get caught that night, who knows which parents may find out that there was drinking at the party and call your mom or dad the next day. So the bottom line is, you gotta put the pros up against the cons before you make a decision. You might decide it's better to fight the temptation than to give in to the peer pressure. If you do decide to give in to the peer pressure, be prepared to accept the consequences.

* * *

Most of the time, teens and adults talk about peer pressure as a problem. But peer pressure is not always negative. Sometimes peer pressure can force us to more carefully evaluate our own values and beliefs. This can often help us to clarify or even change our feelings or positions. Let's say one of your best friends decides to try out for the cheerleading squad at your school and she keeps nagging you to try out with her. Inside, you feel that cheerleading is a dumb thing to do but you don't want to tell her and hurt her feelings. As tryouts approach, you start making excuses about why you can't make it. Your friend finally asks you straight out what your problem is with cheerleading and why you won't try out with her. Then she starts telling you about how she has been looking for something that would force her to get more exercise, give her a chance to hang out with her friends after school, and be fun to do. Cheerleading fits perfectly for her. You never thought about the exercise part, and suddenly you find yourself thinking a little bit differently about what cheerleading might have to offer. If your friend hadn't pressured you, you might never have thought about the good aspects of cheerleading and stuck to your position that cheerleading is only awful. So, peer pressure can sometimes be helpful, not always a problem.

When will racism end? Will people ever get along? *Wilhemina, age 18*

Racism will end when people stop using race as a "crutch" to protect their own self-esteem ("I am better than you") and when they are willing to educate themselves about the value of cultural differences ("I appreciate you for who you are"). The process starts with you, the person in the mirror, because everyone has at least some stereotypes that prevent them from meeting and appreciating people of other races. You can help yourself and others by promoting (1) diversity in your own life, your school, and your community; (2) respect for each person, regardless of race; and (3) the dignity and self-worth of all. Now you might ask, "How do I actually do this?" If you already live in a community and go to a school that is racially diverse, consider yourself lucky. You already have a place where you can speak out to end racism. If your school or community is not diverse, you're going to have to put out more effort. You can begin by talking to your friends and adults at school about your interest in helping to raise consciousness about racism. Panel discussions inviting kids from other schools, field trips to high schools in different communities, and projects such as a "valuing diversity day" are all ways you can help. Not only will you be working toward eliminating racism, but you'll also be learning great leadership skills that will be incredibly valuable in your life.

* * *

Often, people have racial prejudices because of their ignorance and lack of exposure to people of different races. And, it takes a lot of effort to change your way of thinking, especially if you have been brought up with a lot of racial stereotypes. People of different races can, of course, get along, but first they have to have the opportunity to get to know and understand each other. Think about two siblings forced to share the same room. While at first they may not be able to even imagine getting along, once they realize that they are going to have to live together, they often find that not only do they get along but they enjoy each other's company. Of all the things that can work to end racism, motivation is the most important. You've got to want something to make it happen.

If you are in a racially diverse school, do the White kids seem to hang out only with other White kids? And do the African American kids have their own group? And what about the Hispanic or Asian kids? Think about how you might react to finding out that your African American girlfriend is going out with a White guy. Do you think your African American girlfriend is "lucky" because she is dating a White guy? If you yourself are African American, do you think your African American friend is betraying your race by going out with a White guy? If you are White, would you date a Hispanic guy? If you are Asian, do you feel like you are only supposed to date Asian guys? All of these questions speak to the many stereotypes that some teens have about dating.

In many schools that are racially diverse, teens still seem to hang out only with kids of their own race. And, the few who do extend their friendships and dating to other races are often seen as "breaking the rules." The truth is that it is really in the hands of your generation to get rid of the stereotypes and make it a goal to get to know and establish friendships with kids of different races.

Hot Tips

☞ If everyone was the same, life would be really dull. Celebrate differences and learn about other races and cultures. You'll be glad you did.

☞ Does someone not like you because of your skin color? Your ethnic background? Your religion? People who are prejudiced are just plain ignorant! Don't give them the power to hurt you!

☞ Rich kids aren't better than you. There are plenty of kids who will value you no matter how much money your family has. Remember that money doesn't buy happiness.

☞ Kids who make fun of other kids are insecure. If they hassle you, pretend they don't even exist. If you react, they "win."

☞ In spite of the progress we've made, women are still discriminated against in many situations. Speak up if this happens to you!

☞ If you are hiding your smarts and your talents, *stop* it right now! You have the right to be *seen* as the strong, smart, and talented woman you are. And if a guy doesn't like it, too bad for him. He's a fool!!

☞ Don't change your *real* self just to "fit in." It won't work! Find friends who share your values and respect who you truly are.

☞ Never let your friends convince you to do anything that doesn't feel right to you. It's not worth it!

12

My Parents Just Don't Listen.
How Can I Talk to Them?

I used to get along with my parents, but now we argue all the time. They just don't understand me. I can't talk to them; they never listen. I keep promising myself I won't blow up at them, but it never works. They are impossible to deal with. They just won't let me grow up. We don't agree about anything, and they can't deal with the fact that I have different beliefs than they do. Sometimes I just want to stay in my room all by myself, listen to my music, and talk to my friends on the phone. I wish there was a way to make them understand.—*Marcia*

As a teen, how can I get my parents to "let go" of me and let me make decisions for myself? *Laqueena, age 17*

It's hard for parents when children grow up. Rules that made sense when you were younger now need to be changed. It makes sense that you want to take on greater responsibilities for your life. It also makes sense that your parents want you to be successful. You and your parents will certainly not agree 100% of the time about the decisions you are allowed to make on your own. But it's important to talk with them and give them examples of the types of decisions you feel ready to make. One way to do this is to make three lists: (1) a list of decisions you have already successfully made, (2) a list of decisions that you know you are not ready to make, and (3) a list of "negotiable" decisions—decisions that you would like to be able to start making for yourself. Then, have a heart-to-heart talk with your parents and review all your lists. If your list is reasonable, your parents may be willing to compromise. Suggest to your parents that they can act as "advisors" to you on some of the things on your "negotiable" list and that you make these decisions together. When they see that you are being responsible, they may start to allow you to make the final call about more things. The way you approach your parents about wanting to make more decisions in your life will show them the way you will approach other situations in life—with thoughtfulness.

* * *

If you told a secret to your friend and she gave her word not to tell, and the next day she blabbed it to the whole school, would you tell her another secret about you? Your answer would probably be "no way" because she lost your trust. In order for you to tell her anything again, she would need to regain your trust. This same kind of thing can happen with parents. If you have blown your parents' trust because of something you did, then you need to gain it back. You can do this by being really careful to follow their rules, including curfews, so that they see they can trust you again. While there are probably times when you are sure you can bend the rules or get away with something, don't lie to your parents. Catching you in a lie is the quickest way to lose their trust. Another way to regain their trust is to accept the consequences for your behavior. For example, if you broke your curfew, don't make a million excuses. Accept that you might be grounded or restricted. It can also be helpful to learn how to negotiate with your parents. If you present good, solid reasons for wanting additional privileges, parents have been known to bargain. Negotiation is a valuable skill in adulthood, so now is a good time to start. Do not expect to win all the time. Let your parents win sometimes. The more mature your behavior, the more likely your parents will be to let you make your own decisions.

* * *

It's very frustrating when you don't get to make decisions about your own life. Try sitting down with your parents and letting them know that you wish they were more willing to guide you in your efforts to become more independent, rather than doing everything for you or telling you what to do all the time. Let them know that you feel you are at a point where you can handle more responsibility. Give them plenty of examples of how responsible you have been in the past, so that they are less likely to disagree with you too quickly and give you a rap sheet of all the irresponsible things you've ever done. Making your own decisions doesn't mean shutting your parents out completely. Reassure your parents of this by letting them know that you are still willing to accept their guidance and help in developing the skills you need to deal with certain situations. For example, ask your parents if you can reach an agreement together about your curfew. Ask them what they feel is reasonable and then suggest what you think is reasonable. This will make them take you seriously and you will gain points. Keep in mind that your parents' reluctance to "let go" may have more to do with their efforts to protect you from danger than anything else.

What's a good skill in talking to your parents when they just don't listen?
Courtney, age 14

You're not alone! The number one problem teenagers say they have with their parents is that they don't listen. If you want to work on this, then the first thing you have to do is get their attention. Then, you have to be able to communicate a clear message. Being creative will help you get their attention and help you get your message across. For example, you could put your message on a paper airplane and fly it into your parents' room, or print a poster or banner with your question or message on it. Or, send it by e-mail. Some teens say they make regular appointments with their parents to discuss specific issues. For example, right after dinner, they request a 15-minute appointment. Some teens say that a good time to catch their parents and have them listen is when they are driving in the car together. You can also offer to go with them on errands or to walk the dog. Perhaps you can establish weekly "family meetings" where you discuss family matters. Write down the date and time on the calendar or post it on the refrigerator door. No one's allowed to miss these meetings either! Some teens give their parents a quiz after a discussion to see if their parents remember what they said! Whatever creative thing you come up with, remind your parents how important it is for you to feel heard by them, so they need to listen.

* * *

First, sit back and think about *when* you usually try to talk to your parents. Then think about *how* you usually talk to them. Do you talk to them as they are making breakfast, trying to get your brothers or sisters off to school, or rushing to get to work? At times like these, you probably feel you have to shout or demand what you want in order to be heard. Everyone, including parents, has days and times when they cannot hear anything anyone says. Plus, no one, not even parents, listens well when they feel they are being "shouted at" or spoken to in a critical way. How about making an appointment with your parents so that you can sit down together without any distractions? Try to convey your ideas without being critical or making statements like, "You never do this" or "You never listen to anything I say!" Instead, begin your statements with "I think I'm being ignored" or "I feel hurt when you don't listen to what I have to say." And, when you do catch your parents listening to you, let them know that you appreciate it ("Thanks for listening to me, Mom"). If you feel it's too hard to talk to your parents without it ending up in a screaming match, try writing them a letter. Whatever you do, your goal is to communicate in a respectful and non-blaming way. The key here is to use what we call "I" messages. Saying "I feel" or "I need" works a lot better than saying "You don't" or "You never."

* * *

Good communication involves both listening and sharing different points of view. Work with your parents to create "rules for good communication" for the whole family. For example, one rule could be that everyone agrees to take turns talking while the others listen without interruptions or put-downs. It can sometimes help to use a timer so that each person has equal time to talk. Another rule could be that after one person finishes talking, everyone else explains what they thought the speaker meant to be sure that there were no misunderstandings. For example, you might say, "So, you say you're upset about my English grade because you think I didn't do all the homework assignments. Now I'd like to tell you how I think I got that grade." This shows the speaker that they were really heard. But don't forget—good listening does not mean always agreeing. Even after everyone has expressed their points of view, you all might still agree to disagree.

How do I deal with anger during arguments with my parents? *Melissa, age 16*

The first thing you have to do to deal with your anger is to recognize that you are angry. Your body will usually give you some signals that can help you know when you are angry. For example, you may feel your body getting warmer, your jaw getting tighter, or your heart beating faster. Once you know that you *are* angry, try to figure out exactly what is causing you to feel this way. Often times, teens get angry because they want to protect something they value. Maybe you get angry to protect your independence, like when your parents insist on calling your friend's parents before they will let you go out together. Maybe you get angry because you feel misunderstood or unfairly judged, like when you have a teacher who won't give anyone more than a "B" but your parents still criticize you for not working hard enough. So, try to figure out exactly what you are angry about. Then, make sure you can describe what you are angry about clearly enough to explain it to your parents. Then tell them directly. For example, "I'm angry because I want to go to the party on Friday night and you won't let me. You make me feel like a baby." After you have clearly explained what you are angry about, you have a choice to make: either to continue the debate or take a time-out. If you decide on a time-out, tell your parents, "I'm too angry to talk to you right now. I need to cool off." Then you can return to finish the discussion when you feel calmer. Whether you decide to continue the discussion now or later, once you are ready, ask your parents to listen to what you have to say without interrupting you, and then be willing to listen to their point of view without interrupting them. Finally, see if you can compromise. For example, "Would you agree to let me go to the party if you call Lisa's parents first and they tell you that they're going to be there, and I come home by 11:30?" Remember, it's important to be prepared for the possibility that you won't get what you want.

* * *

Nearly every teen girl gets angry with her parents, some more often than others and with more intensity. Now, take a minute to think about what you do when you get angry. There are some things you probably do that are *not* helpful, like saying or doing something that hurts the person you're mad at. While it's natural to want to hurt someone you are frustrated with, it's just not the best thing to do. Lashing out at someone usually makes them want to hurt you back. In the same way, trying to get back at your parents by doing or saying something hurtful may just result in a punishment or restriction. There's another, better strategy to use. This one can be hard to put into practice because you'll have to go against your natural urge to want to lash out. But, if you do it, it can increase your chances of getting what you want.

First, make sure you are calm, cool, and collected. Pretend you are a lawyer trying to convince a jury. Think of the reasons why you want what you want or think what you think. It can help if you write down your arguments first, or go over them with a friend. This will help you organize your thoughts and say what you really mean. Then, present your case, calmly but convincingly. Try hard not to become hot tempered. Your parents are more likely to listen and view you as a mature adolescent if you keep your cool. These steps might get you more of what you want, even if they don't get you all of what you want. Most importantly, using this strategy can lead to a more peaceful and respectful relationship between you and your parents.

* * *

Sometimes, when people get angry, they have a hard time thinking straight, so they say or do things that backfire and make the situation worse. *Feeling* angry in and of itself doesn't get you into trouble. What often *will* get you into trouble is how you act when you are angry (for example, yelling, cursing, slamming doors, throwing things). This is called "venting," and while it may release some of your angry feelings, it certainly won't help you get what you want!

You can manage your anger better by trying some of these techniques. If you feel you cannot continue a conversation because you are way too angry, you might try taking a deep breath and counting to 10 before speaking again. Or make an excuse, like you have to go to the bathroom. Then lock the bathroom door, splash some cold water on your face, and practice in the mirror what you want to say to your parents, like "I feel angry right now because ..." or "I am angry because you never listen to me." When you're ready, put your feet firmly on the ground, walk slowly and calmly back to your parents, and tell them what you want to say. Don't let anything get you off track. If there's just no way you can talk to them, head up to your room, sit down, and put it all in writing. A letter to your parents can make a big difference. Making the decision to handle your anger in a mature and responsible manner will help build your parents' respect, confidence, and trust in you.

What are some ways parents and their adolescents can compromise? *Allie, age 18*

The "key to compromise" is to give up thinking that you have to be right. If you have to be right, there is a strong chance that you will have a power struggle with your parents, with no chance for compromise. The goal of any compromise is to find a course of action or a solution that works best for everyone involved, not to expose who's right and who's wrong. People are more willing to negotiate if they feel that their side has been heard before making the final decision. Therefore, it is important to take the time to really listen to your parents without interrupting them. Then, ask them to do the same for you. If you've listened carefully, you will be able to take the first important step in working out a compromise, which is to determine how far apart you really are on the issue. Don't assume from the start that there will be a huge disagreement just because they are your parents. Also, keep in mind that a compromise doesn't have to be permanent. You can suggest to your parents that you try something for a week or two and see how it goes. Set up a specific time to discuss how the compromise is working out. Then you can decide if it should be made permanent or if further changes are needed.

* * *

Teenagers and parents can both be stubborn. Sometimes, in spite of your efforts to compromise with your parents, it doesn't work: You just can't get your point across, you can't get your way even a bit, and you feel totally frustrated. Well, it's not hopeless. Have you ever heard the saying: "Don't work harder, work smarter"? That means that instead of doing more of the same thing, try something different, something that might work better. If the same old tactics don't work, why keep trying them? If you've already argued, persuaded, pleaded, and begged, and *still* haven't made any progress, it is definitely time to try a different "compromise technique," something new to get your parents to pay attention and listen to your point of view.

Sit down and start by making a list of all the things *you* are willing to compromise. (If you've got a computer, use it.) Are you willing to walk the dog for a month? Are you willing to wash the dishes every night? Are you willing to mow the lawn, wash the car, even serve your parents breakfast in bed? You have to give a little to get a little. So, start by making an offer to your parents. Think of what is important to *them*, and make a commitment to do it. You can even add in some cute or funny stuff, since a little humor can lighten up a tense situation (you could offer to dye your mother's hair purple, for example!). After you've made all your serious and funny offers, ask for what you want in return. Be simple, clear, straightforward, and don't ask for too much all at once or the whole thing will backfire.

Now take your list and leave it for your parents

(or send it to them by e-mail). Or make a greeting card, a design, or a picture that will get their attention. Tape it to the bathroom mirror, or put it on the pillow on their bed, someplace they are sure to see it. But don't nag them—let them have a chance to consider what you've offered and what you want in return. If they don't bring up the issue, wait until a calm moment and ask if they received your message. Hopefully, with a little creativity and humor, you will have gotten your point across and can make some progress toward a compromise. Don't forget, though, you may be dying your mother's hair purple in the morning!

How can I communicate to my parents that I've got different beliefs than they do without getting in a fight and gain their respect and acceptance? *Kimberly, age 17*

Since your beliefs represent who you are, it is understandable that your beliefs are very important to you and that you want your parents to respect them. But here's the tough part. Your "different" beliefs can be threatening to your parents. Even though your beliefs represent your becoming a unique individual, your parents may see them as a rejection of some of the values that they hold sacred, or they may think they are hurtful to you in some way. The fact that you may not see your beliefs in any of these ways is part of the conflict. However, the common values you do share with your parents can help you through your differences.

Try making a list of all the values that you share with your parents. It will probably be a longer list than your differences. The list may include all sorts of shared beliefs, like the importance of love, honesty, kindness, generosity, loyalty, respect, and responsibility. Then, if you communicate your beliefs in a calm and respectful fashion, you are more likely to receive respect back from your parents. When conflicts arise, return to your list of shared values to help your parents see that you still share many of their beliefs. Reminding your parents that you share some of their beliefs can help them accept your different beliefs.

* * *

When you and your parents have different beliefs, it can be very difficult for you to listen to each other. One of the best ways to keep from getting in a fight about your beliefs is to truly listen to what your parents have to say and not just think about your own opinions. Listen to their explanations of their beliefs. Then, when you tell them about your beliefs, do it in a way that respects their right to differ and doesn't try to convince them to believe what you believe. This would be good advice for them too! If you treat your parents' opinions with respect, they are more likely to treat yours with respect!

However, there are some parents who have trouble accepting and allowing their children to have minds of their own. So, as hard as you try, you may not be able to get your parents to accept your right to have your own beliefs. Another problem you may have is that as long as you are living in their house, your parents will have certain expectations. Some of these expectations are supported by the legal system (like going to school). Others involve things that are so important to your parents that they insist on them (like going to church). Regardless of respectful communication and an agreement to disagree, your parents may still choose not to change some of the "rules of the house." At these times, while you probably have to follow their rules, remember that while you may have to *do* certain things, no one can make you *believe* anything.

* * *

From your question, two things are very clear: One is that you *want* your parents' respect and acceptance, and the second is that you'd rather not fight about it. This means that you're on your way to finding some solutions. And, you've already said it—communication is the key. First, think about what you have already tried. When have your parents listened and when have they not listened? Are there particular issues that they really don't seem to get? If you want your parents' respect and acceptance, and they don't seem to hear the way you've been trying to communicate with them, then you may have to look for ways that they *can* hear. It may help to find out a few things about your parents, to get to know them as people who were once kids themselves. Find out if they ever got in trouble, or if they had a hard time being understood by their parents. Initially they might say, "No one ever thought of these things when I was a kid because kids just accepted what their parents told them." I wouldn't completely buy this. However, if you can understand a little more about when they were growing up, then you can try to educate them a little about what your world is like now. Asking your parents about their upbringing can make them feel more open to hearing about your beliefs, because they realize you're not completely blowing off theirs. Keep in mind that as their kids get older, many parents have a lot of fears about things they can't control in their kids' lives. So, be compassionate about how hard it may be for them to realize that you have beliefs that are different from theirs.

Sometimes I am mean to my family for no reason in particular. Why do I do this?
Lisa, age 17

One reason why you might be mean to your family is that you've been hurt or frustrated by a friend or someone outside the family. You don't feel like you can show your anger or hurt feelings directly to the person who hurt you. So, you take it out on your parents because you know they'll always be around. You know they won't reject or abandon you, like you fear might happen if you are mean to your friend. A second reason why you might be mean to your family is to create distance. Your parents probably want to know more about what you're doing and thinking than you want to tell them. Their constant questions can be really annoying. While being mean rarely solves anything, it may make them back off for a while so that you can get the privacy you need. But, at the same time, when your "meanness" erupts, you hurt the people in your family, and afterward you probably don't feel so good about yourself either. When this happens, the best thing you can do is to consider apologizing for your behavior. While apologies can be difficult and require courage, they can also open the door to better communication and allow you and your family to talk openly about what's bothering you. So, even though you might resist the idea, try to apologize when you've been mean. Take a deep breath, and just blurt it out: "I'm sorry for being mean, Mom and Dad." The difficult moment will be over in a couple of seconds, and you'll be relieved. Then, maybe you can talk with them about what is really upsetting you.

* * *

It's a positive start that you are aware that sometimes you are mean to your family for no reason. In psychology, we call this *displaced anger*. It means that sometimes people take out their anger on people who are not the real cause of it. Maybe you are angry at a friend, your boss, or a teacher. But, if you are mean to them, it could really cause big problems. So, you "displace" your anger onto the people you feel safest with—your family. Because you can't express your upset feelings to the people you are really angry at, you may keep your feelings bottled up inside until they end up bubbling over and exploding at the people in your family. Here are two things that can help: One is to simply say to your family, "I'm sorry I was mean to you, it really isn't you I'm mad at," and the second thing to do, if possible, is to find a way of telling the person you are *really* angry at what's bothering you. If you can't tell them directly, it might help to talk it over with a friend or even with one of your parents. Sometimes, simply understanding why you've been mean will make you feel better.

* * *

Being a teenager is a very challenging time in a young woman's life. You are facing many conflicting pressures and responsibilities. This causes stress. It is important to have outlets for your feelings, like friends, teachers, or other adults to talk to about what's going on in your life. This is one good way of coping with your stress. But, when you don't have outlets, you may lash out at the people closest to you, like your family. It's important that you not beat yourself up and say, "what a bad person I am." If you feel you've been mean to someone in your family for no particular reason, go back and apologize to the person, even if it's later. You don't have to go into a long explanation if you don't want to. You can simply say, "I didn't mean to say that stuff to you. I just had a really bad day." Or, you could use this as an opportunity to talk with them about who and what really made you angry. Hopefully, you will be able to feel their support and you both will understand each other better. None of us is perfect. We all make mistakes. The important thing is to learn from your mistakes, and if you think you were wrong, acknowledge it and apologize. It shows how mature you are!

Hot Tips

☞ Anger is normal and healthy. But, if you want your parents to hear you, you'll have to keep your cool. Learn how to manage your anger.

☞ We all make mistakes. Admitting when you are wrong and apologizing goes a long way to making others respect you and see you as a mature person!

☞ Remember, your parents want the best for you even when they are acting like jerks. If you can't talk to them face-to-face, find some other way. You can send them a letter or an e-mail. You might even ask another adult to help you communicate with them.

☞ Of course you don't have exactly the same beliefs as your parents. You are your own person! Instead of shutting them out, try telling them about your position or beliefs. And remember, in the end, you might have to simply agree to disagree.

☞ If you feel your parents don't really listen, you are not alone. Most teens would agree with you. Learn how to be a good listener. Try to communicate with your parents in a calm and respectful manner—don't interrupt them, and offer to take turns talking.

☞ Learning to negotiate and compromise can go a long way toward getting you the things that you want. But, remember that in a compromise, you only get *part* of what you want, not the whole thing.